ALABANZA

ALABANZA

New and Selected Poems 1982–2002

Martín Espada

W. W. Norton & Company

New York London

For information about permission to reproduce selections from this book, write to
Permissions, W. W. Norton & Company, Inc., 500 Fifth Avenue, New York, NY 10110

Manufacturing by The Courier Companies, Inc.
Book design by Chris Welch
Production manager: Anna Oler

Library of Congress Cataloging-in-Publication Data

Espada, Martín, 1957–
Alabanza : new and selected poems 1982–2002 / Martín Espada.—1st ed.

p. cm.

ISBN 0-393-05192-7
1. Hispanic Americans—Poetry. I. Title.
PS3555 .S53 A78 2003

811' .54—dc21   2002152905

W. W. Norton & Company, Inc., 500 Fifth Avenue, New York, N.Y. 10110
www.wwnorton.com

W. W. Norton & Company Ltd., Castle House, 75/76 Wells Street, London W1T 3QT

1 2 3 4 5 6 7 8 9 0

This book is dedicated to my family

CONTENTS

V. from *Imagine the Angels of Bread* (1996)

VI. from *A Mayan Astronomer in Hell's Kitchen* (2000)

VII. *Alabanza: New Poems* (2002)

ACKNOWLEDGMENTS

Some of the new poems included in this collection have appeared or
will appear in the following publications, to whose editors grateful
acknowledgment is made:

El Andar: "Sing Zapatista"
Café Review: "Ezequiel," "The Poet in the Box"
Céide: "Now the Dead will Dance the Mambo"
Hanging Loose: "Alabanza: In Praise of Local 100," "Contemplation"
Hopscotch: "Ezequiel," "The Poet in the Box," "Circle Your Name"
The Massachusetts Review: "Ghazal for Open Hands"
Modern Haiku: "Sheep Haiku"
The Nation: "Alabanza: In Praise of Local 100"
Peacework: "Ghazal for Open Hands"
Photographers, Writers and the American Scene: "Ezequiel"
Ploughshares: "Now the Dead will Dance the Mambo," "Inheritance
    of Waterfalls and Sharks," "The Monsters at the Edge of the
    World," "En la calle San Sebastián"
Poetry Ireland Review: "Offering of Stones"
The Progressive: "Parole Hearing," "Searching for La Revolución in
    the Streets of Tijuana"
Quarterly West: "Offering of Stones"

Sahara: "Sing Zapatista"
U.S. Latino Review: "The Poet in the Box"
Waxwing: "Ghazal for Open Hands"
Worcester Magazine: "Parole Hearing"

Many thanks to Doug Anderson, John Deane, Cola Franzen, Katherine and Klemente Gilbert-Espada, Frances Goldin, the Rubí Theater Company, Camilo Pérez-Bustillo, Leroy Quintana, Ilan Stavans, and Michael Veve for their support.

Gloria a las manos que la mina excavaran.

Gloria a las manos que el ganado cuidaran.

Gloria a las manos que el tabaco, que la caña y el café sembraran . . .

Para ellas y para su patria, ¡alabanza! ¡alabanza!

Glory to the hands that dug the mine.

Glory to the hands that cared for the cattle.

Glory to the hands that planted the tobacco, the sugarcane and the
coffee . . .

For them and for their country, praise! Praise!

—Juan Antonio Corretjer, "Oubao-Moin"

I

from *The Immigrant Iceboy's Bolero* (1982)

Mrs. Báez Serves Coffee on the Third Floor

It hunches
with a brittle black spine
where they poured
gasoline on the stairs
and the banister
and burnt it.

The fire went running
down the steps,
a naked lunatic,
calling the names
of the neighbors,
cackling in the hall.

The immigrants
ate terror with their hands
and prayed to Catholic statues
as the fire company
pumped a million gallons in
and burst the roof,
as an old man
on the top floor
with no name known
to authorities
strangled on the smoke
and stopped breathing.

Some of the people left.
There's a room on the third floor:
high-heeled shoes kicked off,
a broken dresser,
the saint's portrait
hanging where it looked on
shrugging shoulders for years,
soot, trash, burnt tile,
a perfect black lightbulb
to remember everything.

And some stayed. The old men
barechested, squatting
on the milk crates to play dominoes
in the front-stoop sun;
the younger ones, the tigres,
watching the block with unemployed faces
bitter as bad liquor;
Mrs. Báez, who serves coffee
on the third floor
from tiny porcelain cups,
insisting that we stay;
the children who live
between narrow kitchens
and charred metal doors
and laugh anyway;
the skinny man, the one

just arrived from Santo Domingo,
who cannot read or write,
with no hot water
for six weeks,
telling us in the hallway
that the landlord set the fire
and everyone knows it,
the building's worth more empty.

The street organizer said it:
burn the building out,
blacken an old Dominicano's lungs
and sell
so that the money-people
can renovate
and live here
where an old Dominicano died,
over the objections
of his choking spirit.

But some have stayed.
Stayed for the malicious winter,
stayed frightened of the white man who comes
to collect rent
and borrowing from cousins
to pay it,
stayed waiting for the next fire,

and the siren,
hysterical and late.

Someone poured gasoline
on the steps outside her door,
but Mrs. Báez
still serves coffee
in porcelain cups
to strangers,
coffee the color
of a young girl's skin
in Santo Domingo.

Cordillera

Far from beggars' hands
searching in cities
of Iberian cobblestone,
the mountains rest,
a council of elders
drowsing in the market square.

The rain forests are steaming
and sluggish, green palm
and broken rock
broad like the cheekbones
of an extinct people.

Older than suffering:

the mountains are shamans,
guarding the caves
from archaeologists;
the mountains are guerrilleros,
rising together
to swallow terrified armies;
the mountains are peasants,
great shoulders breaking the earth
to spring forth crops.

Lares, Jayuya, Utuado,
towns of the mountain

where rebellion's song wept
like slaves in the joy
of abolition,
rang like a machete forged
by insurgent blacksmiths,
raged like a rainstorm
deep in the chest of mountains.

We are of mountains.

Descended from
Taíno carvings,
Spanish watchtowers,
African manacles,
the jíbaro plow,

the only glimpse
a Victorian photograph
of minor officials,
shirtsleeved and tough;
a brick from the house
where my father was born.

I will disappear
in Borinquen's mountains,
lost among boulders,
drinking from

mottled creekbeds,
exploring unknown gardens,
discovering hungry shacks
and wild sow
in green plátano thicket,
searching, like those
beggars' hands,
for bread and sight
and salvation.

Tato Hates the New York Yankees
for Frank Espada

It was 1947.
Tato was getting a tryout
with the New York Yankees.

The only Puerto Rican
allowed on the neighborhood team,
he always stayed for the fight
after the game, shouts
and the skidding of spikes
on asphalt.

He was seventeen years old,
a brownskinned boy
with big hands
who oiled his glove every day.
He could see the seams
on the ball
from four hundred feet;
he could hit it
into the distance
with a sweeping grace.
From the batting cage
he could wallop a white blur
to ricochet
off a stadium billboard
or the pitcher's leg.

The scout told Tato
he had the most natural swing
since Ted Williams.

He almost had a tryout
with the New York Yankees,
but the alarm clock
didn't work that morning.

It was the spring of 1947.
There were no brownskinned boys
in the American League.

And the New York Yankees
gave no more tryouts;
they broadcast the message sent
by overdue bills
and losing lottery tickets.

Tato still played ball.
He had to.
He still had that swing,
and he had to hit
something.

He played semipro,
the industrial leagues,

first base
for the tool and die company,
stealing home
in the crippled old stadium
outside Jersey City—
the pitcher had this crazy windup,
so he just left third
and walked across the plate—
remembering, in front
of the ballgame on TV,
how the white guys
put the spikes in his neck
on the double play,
fifteen dollars a night
and a bus ride
to the waterfront towns.

Then he was working
graveyard shift
with a sanitation crew
on the Holland Tunnel,
soaping his illusions
off the walls.

I wasn't good enough,
he says today, but the words
are cheated bettors at the track.

No one calls him Tato anymore,
and he hates the New York Yankees.

Heart of Hunger

Smuggled in boxcars through fields of dark morning,
tied to bundles at railroad crossings,
the brown grain of faces dissolved in bus station dim,
immigrants: mexicano, dominicano,
guatemalteco, puertorriqueño, orphans and travelers,
refused permission to use gas station toilets,
beaten for a beer in unseen towns with white porches,
or evaporated without a tombstone in the peaceful grass,
a centipede of hands moving,
hands clutching infants that grieve,
fingers to the crucifix,
hands that labor.

Long past backroads paved with solitude,
hands in the thousands reach for the crop-ground together,
the countless roots of a tree lightning-torn,
capillaries running to a heart of hunger,
tobaccopicker, grapepicker, lettucepicker.

Obscured in the towering white clouds of cities in winter,
thousands are bowing to assembly lines,
frenzied in kitchens and sweatshops,
mopping the vomit of others' children,
leaning into the iron's steam
and the steel mill glowing.

Yet there is a pilgrimage,
a history straining its arms and legs,
an inexorable striving,
shouting in Spanish
at the police of city jails
and border checkpoints,
mexicano, dominicano,
guatemalteco, puertorriqueño,
fishermen wading into the North American gloom
to pull a fierce gasping life
from the polluted current.

Jim's Blind Blues

in memoriam

There are some things
doctors can't fix,
his brother said.
Heroin and diabetes.

Squatting naked on the mattress,
he tells seeing-eye dog jokes
through a smirk,
face swollen and sleepy
with the geography of attempted suicide,
his laugh a jazzman's funeral,
a sneering clarinet.

Don't say anything,
but his veins have collapsed
so he shoots it
in his neck,
his brother said.

The unclean needle
bit sores into his marrow,
pus where the skin split,
and now he stinks
like a dress rehearsal
for the cemetery.
Going blind
by the window

in his brother's apartment,
he fumbles
through the medicine bottles
for the radio.

We're gonna drive
cross-country.
See this country.
Before his eyesight goes,
his brother said,
ex-convict brother,
hundred-dollar-a-week brother,
caretaker brother.

A junkie
is going to the place
where secrets
are auctioned into slavery
and shadows
sell the darkness to each other.

Here, adrift in the undertow of that darkness,
down in night's black whirlpool,
his brother
will not know
where to find him.

Power

Crazyman
arms up
in the inter-
section to stop
traffic
didn't notice
that the light
was red
anyway

II

from *Trumpets from the Islands of Their Eviction* (1987)

Trumpets from the Islands of Their Eviction

At the bar two blocks away,
immigrants with Spanish mouths
hear trumpets
from the islands of their eviction.
The music swarms into the barrio
of a refugee's imagination,
along with predatory squad cars
and bullying handcuffs.

Their eviction:
like Mrs. Alfaro, evicted
when she trapped ten mice,
sealed them in plastic sandwich bags
and gifted them to the landlord;
like Daniel, the boy stockaded
in the back of retarded classrooms
for having no English
to comfort third-grade teachers;
like my father years ago,
brown skin darker than the Air Force uniform
that could not save him, seven days county-jailed
for refusing the back of a Mississippi bus;
like the nameless Florida jíbaro
the grocery stores would not feed
in spite of the dollars he showed,
who returned with a machete,
collected cans from shelves

and forced the money
into the clerk's reluctant staring hand.

We are the one identified by case number,
summons in the wrong language,
judgment without stay of execution.
Mrs. Alfaro has ten days
to bundle the confusion of five children
down claustrophobic stairs
and away from the apartment.

And at the bar two blocks away,
immigrants with Spanish mouths
hear trumpets
from the islands of their eviction.
The sound scares away devils
like tropical fish
darting between the corals.

Toque de queda: Curfew in Lawrence

Lawrence, Massachusetts, 1984

Now the archbishop comes to Lawrence
to say a Spanish mass.
But the congregation understands
without translation:
the hammering of the shoe factory,
sweating fever of infected August,
housing projects' asylum chatter,
dice on the sidewalk,
saints at the window,
two days' pollution of riot-smoke,
the mayor's denials.

Toque de queda: curfew signs
outlaw the conspiracy of foreign voices at night.
Barricades surround the buildings
widow-black from burning, collapsed in shock.
After the explosion of shotgun pellets
and shattered windshields,
sullen quiet stands watching on Tower Hill,
trash, brick and bottle fragments
where the arrested kneeled, hands clapped
to the neck, and bodies with Spanish names
slammed into squad cars, then disappeared.

The mobs are gone: white adolescents
who chanted *USA* and flung stones
at the scattering of astonished immigrants,

ruddy faces slowing the car to shout *spic*
and wave beer cans.

Now the archbishop comes to Lawrence
to say a Spanish mass.
At the housing projects where they are kept,
they're collecting money for bail.

Tiburón

East 116th
and a long red car
stalled with the hood up
roaring salsa
like a prize shark
mouth yanked open
and down in the stomach
the radio
of the last fisherman
still tuned
to his lucky station

El señor está muerto

He was Paco the gambler,
Francisco the bookkeeper in three languages,
Papito the generous grandfather of Tres Reyes.
He was ninety years old,
his fluttering swollen hand
would pull the oxygen mask away,
and he howled all night for morphine,
for water he could not swallow.

Sporadic rain scattered on leaves and sheets of tin roof,
fragile shacks and trees leaning distant in hospital window.
His son and grandson passed shards of coffee-soaked bread,
one keeping vigil while the other did not sleep
on the mattress. The night was a dark
wounded animal, the scrape of forced breath
and laboring ribs heard from the corner.
Twice they yelled for morphine when the moans were too strong,
then were told a man so weak would lose
the last palpitations of the heart with a painkilling drug.
In the morning, his eyes were white boats overturned,
blind yet amazed at hallucinations, at a sight
through the ceiling. An orderly greeted him
and squirted juice in the dry gaping mouth.

He was still living when they left. Later that morning,
his son and grandson sat at the funeral business
surrounded by steel coffins docked in waiting.

A stranger from the next room called:
The hospital words were recited by telephone
with medical apology, then the son loudly reported
el señor está muerto—the gentleman is dead—
and the son's body huge with a father's life
lowered to a leather chair.
He spoke: a plain coffin would be carried without religion
to the city cemetery tomorrow afternoon.
Signing the burial papers, a sob struck the back of his head,
caught between the eyes with his fingers.

An uncle, a man once a priest eulogized,
Francisco Espada era un hombre contento,
porque durante su vida tenía la oportunidad de dar:
Francisco Espada was a contented man,
for during his life he had the opportunity to give.
Those who knew the giving, the serious children
of grandfather Papito, the old women mouths creased
with the remembered gifts of Paco the gambler
fifty years ago, all became the dark march
approaching a grave too fresh for the headstone.

The moist red earth was plowed aside, son and grandson
pallbearers for a coffin surprisingly light, gripping the rails
against a white sky that almost rained.

From an Island You Cannot Name

Thirty years ago,
your linen-gowned father stood
in the dayroom of the VA hospital,
grabbing at the plastic
identification bracelet
marked *Negro*,
shouting *I'm not!*
Take it off!
I'm Other!

The Army photograph
pinned to your mirror
says he was,
Black, Negro,
dark as West Indian rum.

And this morning,
daughter of a man
from an island you cannot name,
you gasp tears
trying to explain
that you're Other,
that you're not.

Mariano Explains Yanqui Colonialism to Judge Collings

Judge: Does the prisoner understand his rights?
Interpreter: ¿Entiende usted sus derechos?
Prisoner: *¡Pa'l carajo!*
Interpreter: Yes.

Again the Mercenaries: Atlantic Coast of Nicaragua, 4th of July 1982

The Río Sucio drags the reaching brown hand of branches
away from a shoreline of trees,
current quickened like the pulse of furious veins
spreading darkness over the cocodrilo's rough back.
Here dusk is a mulato, night the grandson
of a slave, walking the river into mines
collapsed like the caverns of an exhausted lung.
The whites took the gold and left tuberculosis
says El Indio, maneuvering the jeep,
and again the mercenaries
have gathered their muddy shadows close to the river,
paid with the rifles and lead of a distant empire.

From this nameless road a truck is thrown,
side-sprawled, underbelly still warm iron,
and approaching three unknown men swaggering machetes.

La tormenta

La muerte es una tormenta.
Death is a storm,
he said.
And the village
is an anthill scattering.
Héctor in the Army
of El Salvador:
conscripted at fourteen,
a deserter three years later.

A boy with wide ears
and one shirt,
he walked across Guatemala,
México and Arizona to get here,
almost swallowed
too much river and mud
at the border.
He wants to be called Tony
in the United States.

In the basement,
partway through
translated instructions
on where he will eat today,
Tony pulls the hood
of a big borrowed coat
over his head and bodyrocks,

a monk shadowboxing
at the clang of churchbells,
moving to a song
with a distant helicopter beat,
la tormenta
and the anthill scattering.

The Right Hand of a Mexican Farmworker in Somerset County, Maryland

A rosary tattoo
between thumb
and forefinger
means that
every handful
of crops and dirt
is a prayer,
means that Christ
had hard hands
too

Leo Blue's and the Tiger Rose

Mitchell walked three miles
for cigarettes
and a telephone call to Legal Aid:
take me away from Leo Blue's,
he said.

Labor camp: tin shacks and a sand pit,
gathering place for apparitions
killed by the heat;
through the tin surface and screens
the sun crawls like a bright spider
that startles the eyes and heart,
a sweat-demon slowly walking.

This is a row of darkskinned men
with old shoes,
recruited from the mission shelter
in Tampa, drink-poisoned then,
still blurred;
a swallow of Tiger Rose wine
before cucumber picking
in the swollen light of morning.
They dump cucumber buckets
for another swallow
of the craved wine
from a crewleader's truck.

All day bending
like something storm-broken
and left to sway,
dream scarecrows
with stiff hands picking.
Ten hours gone.

Return to camp,
back to the crewleader's gospel music tapes
loudly preaching,
minimum wage signs no one can read
posted in the kitchen,
camp meals of pigs' ears and pinto beans
deducted with brown pay-envelope arithmetic:
Mitchell works three days
for six dollars.
We wait
as he soaps the farmer's car
to pay for the last
of his meals.

We leave the brilliance of sharp-angled roof,
old shoes unclaimed
near hunchback-mattress.

Watch Me Swing

I was the fifth man hired
for the city welfare cleaning crew
at the old Paterson Street ballpark,
Class A minor leagues.
Opening Day was over,
and we raked the wooden benches
for the droppings of the crowd:
wrappers, spilled cups, scorecards,
popcorn cartons, chewed and spat hot dogs,
a whiskey bottle, a condom dried on newspaper.

We swung our brooms,
pausing to watch home runs sail
through April imagination
over the stone fence three hundred feet away,
baseball cracking off the paint factory sign
across Washington Street.
We shuffled and kicked,
plowed and pushed
through the clinging garbage,
savoring our minimum wages.

When the sweeping was done,
and the grandstand benches
clean as Sunday morning pews,
the team business manager
inspected the aisles,

reviewed the cleaning crew
standing like broomstick cadets
and said:
We only need four.
I was the fifth man hired.

As the business manager
strode across the outfield
back to his office,
I wanted to leap the railing,
crouch at home plate
and swing my broom,
aiming a smacked baseball
for the back of his head,
yelling *watch me swing, boss,*
watch me swing.

The Moon Shatters on Alabama Avenue

A wooden box rattled
with coins for the family,
on a stoop where the roots
of a brown bloodstain grew.

Brooklyn, 1966: Agropino Bonillo was his name,
a neighbor, the yellow leaflet said,
a kitchen worker who walked home
under the scaffolding of trains at night,
hurrying past streetlamps with dark eyes.
He was there when the boys surrounded him,
quick with shouts and pushing,
addiction's hunger in a circle.
When he had no money,
the kicking began.

The mourners clustered at the storefront,
then marched between cadaverous buildings
down Alabama Avenue,
as the night turned blue with rain
in a heavy sky of elevated track.
The first candles struggled, smothered wet;
onlookers leaned warily as they watched.
A community of faces gathered and murmured
in the dim circles of light,
kept alive by cupped hands.

In the asphalt street polished black by rain
and windows where no one was seen
hesitant candles appeared, a pale blur started
on the second floor, another trembling glimmer
slipped to the back of the march, then more,
multiplied into a constellation
spreading over the sidewalk,
a swarm of candles that throbbed descending
tenement steps in the no longer absolute dark,
as if the moon had shattered
and dropped in burning white pieces
on the night.

His name was Agropino Bonillo,
spoken remembering
every sixty-dollar week
he was bent in the kitchen,
his children
who could not dress for winter
and brawled against welfare taunts
at the schoolyard,
the unlit night
that the sweep of legs was stopped
by his belly and his head.

And the grief of thousands illuminated city blocks,
moving with the tired feet of the poor:

candles a reminder of the wakes too many and too soon,
the frustrated prayers and pleading with saints,
in memoriam for generations of sacrificed blood
warm as the wax sticking to their fingers,
and years of broken streetlamps, bowed
with dark eyes, where addiction's hunger waits nervously.

Over the wooden box, a woman's face
was slick in a drizzle of tears.
Her hand dropped coins like seed.

III

from *Rebellion is the Circle of a Lover's Hands* (1990)

La tumba de Buenaventura Roig

for my great-grandfather, died 1941

Buenaventura Roig,
once peasants in the thousands
streamed down hillsides
to witness the great eclipse
of your funeral.
Now your bones have drifted
with the tide of steep grass,
sunken in the chaos of weeds
bent and suffering
like canecutters in the sun.
The drunken caretaker
cannot find the grave,
squinting at your name,
spitting as he stumbles
between the white Christs
with hands raised
sowing their field
of white crosses.

Buenaventura Roig,
in Utuado you built the stone bridge
crushed years later by a river
raving like a forgotten god;
here sweat streaked your face
with the soil of coffee,
the ground where your nephew slept
while rain ruined the family crop,

and his blood flowered like flamboyán
on the white suit of his suicide.

Buenaventura Roig,
in the town plaza where you were mayor,
where there once was a bench
with the family name,
you shouted subversion
against occupation armies and sugarcane-patrones
to the jíbaros who swayed
in their bristling dry thicket of straw hats,
who knew bundles and sacks
loaded on the fly-bitten beast
of a man's back.

Buenaventura Roig,
not enough money for a white Christ,
lost now even to the oldest gravedigger,
the one with an English name
descended from the pirates of the coast,
who grabs for a shirt-pocket cigarette
as he remembers your funeral,
a caravan trailing in the distance
of the many years
that cracked the skin around his eyes.

Buenaventura Roig,
we are small among mountains,
and we listen for your voice
in the peasant chorus of five centuries,
waiting for the cloudburst of wild sacred song,
pouring over the crypt-wreckage of graveyard,
over the plaza and the church
where the statue of San Miguel
still chokes the devil with a chain.

Rebellion is the Circle of a Lover's Hands
(Pellín and Nina)

for the 50th anniversary
of the Ponce Massacre

The marchers gathered, Nationalists
massed beneath the delicate white balconies
of Marina Street,
and the colonial governor
pronounced the order with patrician calm:
fifty years of family history
says it was Pellín
who dipped a finger
into the bloody soup of his own body
and scratched defiance
in jagged wet letters on the sidewalk.
Around him stormed
the frenzied clattering drumbeat
of machine guns,
the stampede of terrified limbs
and the panicked wail
that rushed babbling
past his dim senses.

Palm Sunday, 1937:
the news
halted the circular motion
of his lover's hands
as she embroidered
the wedding dress.
She nodded, knew
before she was told.

Years later, with another family
in a country of freezing spring rain
called Nueva York,
Nina is quietly nervous
when her son speaks of rifles
in a bullhorn shout,
when coffins are again bobbing
on the furious swell of hands and shoulders,
and the whip of nightsticks
brings fresh blood
stinging from the scalp.

But rebellion
is the circle of a lover's hands,
that must keep moving,
always weaving.

The Savior is Abducted in Puerto Rico

Adjuntas, Puerto Rico, 1985

At a place in the mountains,
where the road skids
into tangled trees
and stacks of rock,
a single white cross leans.

The name has dissolved,
obscured in a century of storms
that asphyxiated shacks
with mud, yanking
the stone vertebrae
from bridges.

On the cross,
the dark absence of Christ
spreads and hangs,
a crucified shadow
where thieves
tore the brass body down,
leaving amputated feet and hands
still nailed,
and the accidental dead
without a guide
on the mountain roads
of the underworld.

Colibrí

for Katherine, one year later

In Jayuya,
the lizards scatter
like a fleet of green canoes
before the invader.
The Spanish conquered
with iron and words:
Indio Taíno for the people
who took life
from the rain
that rushed through trees
like evaporating arrows,
who left the rock carvings
of eyes and mouths
in perfect circles of amazement.

So the hummingbird
was christened *colibrí.*
Now the colibrí
darts and bangs
between the white walls
of the hacienda,
a racing Taíno heart
frantic as if hearing
the bellowing god of gunpowder
for the first time.

The colibrí
becomes pure stillness,
seized in the paralysis
of the prey,
when your hands
cup the bird
and lift him
through the red shutters
of the window,
where he disappears
into a paradise of sky,
a nightfall of singing frogs.

If only history
were like your hands.

Bully

Boston, Massachusetts, 1987

In the school auditorium,
the Theodore Roosevelt statue
is nostalgic
for the Spanish-American war,
each fist lonely for a saber
or the reins of anguish-eyed horses,
or a podium to clatter with speeches
glorying in the malaria of conquest.

But now the Roosevelt school
is pronounced *Hernández*.
Puerto Rico has invaded Roosevelt
with its army of Spanish-singing children
in the hallways,
brown children devouring
the stockpiles of the cafeteria,
children painting Taíno ancestors
who leap naked across murals.

Roosevelt is surrounded
by all the faces
he ever shoved in eugenic spite
and cursed as mongrels, skin of one race,
hair and cheekbones of another.

Once Marines tramped
from the newsreel of his imagination;
now children plot to spray graffiti
in parrot-brilliant colors
across the Victorian mustache
and monocle.

The New Bathroom Policy
at English High School

The boys chatter Spanish
in the bathroom
while the principal
listens from his stall

The only word he recognizes
is his own name
and this constipates him

So he decides
to ban Spanish
in the bathrooms

Now he can relax

Portrait of a Real Hijo de Puta
for Michael

Not the obscenity,
but a real ten year old
son of a whore,
locked out of the apartment
so mamá could return
to the slavery
of her ancestors
who knew the master's burglary
of their bodies at night,
mamá who sleeps
in a pool of clear rum;

and the real hijo de puta poses
with the swim team photograph
at the community center,
bragging fists in the air,
grinning like a cheerleader
with hidden cigarette burns,
a circus strongman
who steals cheese and crackers
from the office
where the door is deliberately
left open.

Cheo Saw an Angel on Division Street

Cheo was a Latin King,
but tomorrow he jumps a bus
for the winter country,
away from the city,
with a vision of the barrio
that will glow
at every gas station
along the smooth night
of the highway.

Cheo saw an angel
on Division Street today:
wandering the block
in the wrong gang colors,
condemned by a sickle of inquisitors,
baptized in gasoline,
purified with a match,
shrieking angel, burning heretic,
brilliant crucifix
thrown through a skylight
on the roof.

And when the chorus of glass
exploded in crescendo,
Cheo heard the angel say:

I am the heat that will flush your face,
I am the sweat of your skin,
I am the one you will pray for,
I am the kiss of the cross.

Latin Night at the Pawnshop

Chelsea, Massachusetts,
Christmas, 1987

The apparition of a salsa band
gleaming in the Liberty Loan
pawnshop window:

Golden trumpet,
silver trombone,
congas, maracas, tambourine,
all with price tags dangling
like the city morgue ticket
on a dead man's toe.

Two Mexicanos Lynched in Santa Cruz, California, May 3, 1877

More than the moment
when forty gringo vigilantes
cheered the rope
that snapped two Mexicanos
into the grimacing sleep of broken necks,

more than the floating corpses,
trussed like cousins of the slaughterhouse,
dangling in the bowed mute humility
of the condemned,

more than the Virgen de Guadalupe
who blesses the brownskinned
and the crucified,
or the guitar-plucking skeletons
they will become
on the Día de los Muertos,

remain the faces of the lynching party:
faded as pennies from 1877, a few stunned
in the blur of execution,
a high-collar boy smirking, some peering
from the shade of bowler hats, but all
crowding into the photograph.

Revolutionary Spanish Lesson

Whenever my name
is mispronounced,
I want to buy a toy pistol,
put on dark sunglasses,
push my beret to an angle,
comb my beard to a point,
hijack a busload
of Republican tourists
from Wisconsin,
force them to chant
anti-American slogans
in Spanish,
and wait
for the bilingual SWAT team
to helicopter overhead,
begging me
to be reasonable

The Intelligence of Scavengers
Atlantic Coast of Nicaragua, 1982

Three vultures walk the ground clumsily
and hunch their wings
like renegade colonels
in rustling cloaks, in full-dress uniform.

They know the geography
of every ambush, the troop movements
of the mercenaries,
turning with an alert salute
of their beaks
to the many beckoning hands
of open graves.

The intelligence of scavengers
is everywhere in the countryside,
patiently scouting the moment
to skin the dead,
to parade arrogantly
among the living.

After the Flood in Chinandega
July, 1982

Nicaragua
is a young brown girl
standing in the mud
of a refugee camp,
grinning at the way
her green bird
balances himself
on her head

The Saint Vincent de Paul Food Pantry Stomp

Madison, Wisconsin, 1980

Waiting for the carton of food
given with Christian suspicion
even to agency-certified charity cases
like me,
thin and brittle
as uncooked linguini,
anticipating the factory-damaged cans
of tomato soup, beets, three-bean salad
in a welfare cornucopia,
I spotted a squashed dollar bill
on the floor, and with
a Saint Vincent de Paul food pantry stomp
pinned it under my sneaker,
tied my laces meticulously,
and stuffed the bill in my sock
like a smuggler of diamonds,
all beneath the plaster statue wingspan
of Saint Vinnie,
who was unaware
of the dance
named in his honor
by a maraca shaker
in the salsa band
of the unemployed.

Federico's Ghost

The story is
that whole families of fruitpickers
still crept between the furrows
of the field at dusk,
when for reasons of whiskey or whatever
the cropduster plane sprayed anyway,
floating a pesticide drizzle
over the pickers
who thrashed like dark birds
in a glistening white net,
except for Federico,
a skinny boy who stood apart
in his own green row,
and, knowing the pilot
would not understand in Spanish
that he was the son of a whore,
instead jerked his arm
and thrust an obscene finger.

The pilot understood.
He circled the plane and sprayed again,
watching a fine gauze of poison
drift over the brown bodies
that cowered and scurried on the ground,
and aiming for Federico,
leaving the skin beneath his shirt
wet and blistered,
but still pumping his finger at the sky.

After Federico died,
rumors at the labor camp
told of tomatoes picked and smashed at night,
growers muttering of vandal children
or communists in camp,
first threatening to call Immigration,
then promising every Sunday off
if only the smashing of tomatoes would stop.

Still tomatoes were picked and squashed
in the dark,
and the old women in camp
said it was Federico,
laboring after sundown
to cool the burns on his arms,
flinging tomatoes
at the cropduster
that hummed like a mosquito
lost in his ear,
and kept his soul awake.

The Florida Citrus Growers Association Responds to a Proposed Law Requiring Handwashing Facilities in the Fields

An orange,
squeezed on the hands,
is an adequate substitute
for soap and water

Jorge the Church Janitor Finally Quits

Cambridge, Massachusetts, 1989

No one asks
where I am from,
I must be
from the country of janitors,
I have always mopped this floor.
Honduras, you are a squatter's camp
outside the city
of their understanding.

No one can speak
my name,
I host the fiesta
of the bathroom,
stirring the toilet
like a punchbowl.
The Spanish music of my name
is lost
when the guests complain
about toilet paper.

What they say
must be true:
I am smart,
but I have a bad attitude.

No one knows
that I quit tonight,

maybe the mop
will push on without me,
sniffing along the floor
like a crazy squid
with stringy gray tentacles.
They will call it Jorge.

IV

from *City of Coughing and Dead Radiators* (1993)

The Hidalgo's Hat and a Hawk's Bell of Gold

Columbus hallucinated gold
wherever sunlight darted
from rock to water, spelled the word
slowly in his logbook
so that the Lord might see
and blow his ship
into a storm of gleaming dust.
When God would not puff his cheeks
for trade winds of gold, the Admiral flourished
a decree on parchment: a hawk's bell
full of gold from every Indio
where the rivers gilded the soil
of Española, 1495.

The Indios could only load the bells
with mirrored sunlight. For bells
without gold, the hands were pressed together
as if in prayer, gripped on the block,
then the knobs of wrists were splintered
by a bright and heavy sword.
Their stumps became torches
seething flames of blood,
the vowels of their language
lamentations flattening the tongue.

While the Admiral slept
in the exhaustion of dysentery,

or amused the Queen
with his zoo of shackled caciques,
the town he named Isabela
dissolved into the stones
like a rumor of gold, deserted swampground.
There is a spirit legend:
that the moans of men in rusting helmets
would radiate from the vine-matted walls,
starved with a mouthful of bark
or mad with a brain soaking in syphilis,
or digging an arrowhead from the eye
fired by an Indio with two hands.

Someone saw the hidalgos there, ghosts of noblemen
bowing in a row, a swirl of velvet cloaks.
As each swept off his feathered hat
in greeting, his head unscrewed
from the hollow between caped shoulders,
swinging in the hat
like a cannonball in a sack.

The Lover of a Subversive is Also a Subversive
for Vilma

The lover of a subversive
is also a subversive.
The painter's compañero was a conspirator,
revolutionary sentenced
to haunt the catacombs of federal prison
for the next half-century.
When she painted her canvas
on the beach, the FBI man
squatted behind her
on the sand, muddying his dark gray suit
and kissing his walkie-talkie,
a pallbearer who missed
the funeral train.

The painter who paints a subversive
is also a subversive.
In her portrait of him, she imagines
his long black twist of hair. In her portraits
of herself, she wears a mask
or has no mouth. She must sell the canvases,
for the FBI man ministered solemnly
to the principal at the school
where she once taught.

The woman who grieves for a subversive
is also a subversive.
The FBI man is a pale-skinned apparition

staring in the market.
She could reach for him
and only touch a pillar of ash
where the dark gray suit had been.
If she hungers to touch her lover,
she must brush her fingers
on moist canvas.

The lover of a subversive
is also a subversive.
When the beach chilled cold,
and the bright stumble of tourists
deserted, she and the FBI man
were left alone with their spying glances,
as he waited calmly
for the sobbing to begin,
and she refused to sob.

Coca-Cola and Coco Frío

On his first visit to Puerto Rico,
island of family folklore,
the fat boy wandered
from table to table
with his mouth open.
At every table, some great-aunt
would steer him with cool spotted hands
to a glass of Coca-Cola.
One even sang to him, in all the English
she could remember, a Coca-Cola jingle
from the forties. He drank obediently, though
he was bored with this potion, familiar
from soda fountains in Brooklyn.

Then, at a roadside stand off the beach, the fat boy
opened his mouth to coco frío, a coconut
chilled, then scalped by a machete
so that a straw could inhale the clear milk.
The boy tilted the green shell overhead
and drooled coconut milk down his chin;
suddenly, Puerto Rico was not Coca-Cola
or Brooklyn, and neither was he.

For years afterward, the boy marveled at an island
where the people drank Coca-Cola
and sang jingles from World War II
in a language they did not speak,

while so many coconuts in the trees
sagged heavy with milk, swollen
and unsuckled.

Who Burns for the Perfection of Paper

At sixteen, I worked after high school hours
at a printing plant
that manufactured legal pads:
Yellow paper
stacked seven feet high
and leaning
as I slipped cardboard
between the pages,
then brushed red glue
up and down the stack.
No gloves: fingertips required
for the perfection of paper,
smoothing the exact rectangle.
Sluggish by 9 P.M., the hands
would slide along suddenly sharp paper,
and gather slits thinner than the crevices
of the skin, hidden.
Then the glue would sting,
hands oozing
till both palms burned
at the punchclock.

Ten years later, in law school,
I knew that every legal pad
was glued with the sting of hidden cuts,
that every open lawbook
was a pair of hands
upturned and burning.

City of Coughing and Dead Radiators

Chelsea, Massachusetts

I cannot evict them
from my insomniac nights,
tenants in the city of coughing
and dead radiators.
They bang the radiators
like cold hollow marimbas;
they cry out
to unseen creatures
skittering across their feet
in darkness;
they fold hands over plates
to protect food
from ceilings black with roaches.

And they answer the call
of the list,
all evictions in court,
brays the clerk.
Quiet and dutiful
as spectral troops returning,
they file into the courtroom,
crowding the gallery:
the patient one from El Salvador,
shoemakers' union refugee,
slapping his neck
to show where that vampire
of an Army bullet

pierced his uncle's windpipe;
the red-haired woman
with no electricity
but the drug's heat
swimming in the pools
of her blue bruises,
whiteskinned as the candles
she lives by,
who will move this afternoon
for a hundred dollars;
the prostitute swollen
with pregnancy and sobbing
as the landlady
sneers *miscarriage*
before a judge
poking his broken hearing aid;
the girl surrounded by a pleading carousel
of children, in Spanish bewilderment,
sleepless and rat-vigilant,
who wins reluctant extermination
but loses the youngest,
lead paint retarded;
the man alcohol-puffed,
graph of scars
stretching across his belly,
locked out, shirt stolen,
arrested at the hearing

for the rampage
of his detox hallucinations;
the Guatemalan boy, who listens
through the wall
for his father's landlord-defiant staccato,
jolted awake
by flashes of the landlord
floating over the bed,
parade balloon
waving a kitchen knife.

For all those sprawled down stairs
with the work boot's crusted map
printed on the back,
the creases of the judge's face
collapse into a fist.
As we shut files
and click briefcases
to leave,
a loud-faced man
trumpets from the gallery:
Death to Legal Aid.

Courthouse Graffiti for Two Voices

Jimmy C.
Greatest Car Thief Alive
Chelsea '88

Then what
are you doing
here?

Mi Vida: Wings of Fright
Chelsea, Massachusetts, 1987

The refugee's run
across the desert borderlands
carved wings of fright
into his forehead,
growing more crooked
with every eviction notice
in this waterfront city of the north.

He sat in the office for the poor,
daughter burrowed asleep
on one shoulder,
and spoke to the lawyer
with a voice trained obedient
in the darkness of church confessionals
and police barracks, Guatemalan dusk.

The lawyer nodded through papers,
glancing up only when the girl awoke
to spout white vomit on the floor
and her father's shirt.
Mi vida: My life, he said,
then said again, as he bundled her
to the toilet.
This was how the lawyer,
who, like the fortune-teller,
had a bookshelf of prophecy

but a cabinet empty of cures,
found himself
kneeling on the floor
with a paper towel.

The Broken Window of Rosa Ramos

Chelsea, Massachusetts, 1991

Rosa Ramos could spread her palm
at the faucet for hours
without cold water
ever hissing hot,
while the mice darted
like runaway convicts
from a hole in the kitchen floor.

The landlord was a spy,
clicking his key in the door unheard
to haunt the living room,
peeking for the thrill of young skin,
a pasty dead-faced man still hungry.

Her husband was dead.
She knew this
from *El Vocero* newspaper,
the picture of his grinning face
sprayed with the black sauce of blood,
a bullet-feast.
Rosa shows his driver's license,
a widow's identification,
with the laminated plastic
cracking across his eyes,
so that he watches her
through a broken window.

She leaves the office
rehearsing with the lawyer
new words in English
for the landlord:
Get out. Get out. Get out.

The Legal Aid Lawyer Has an Epiphany

Chelsea, Massachusetts

When I bounced off the bus for work
at Legal Aid this morning,
I found the spiky halo of a hole
in the front window of the office,
as if some drunk had rammed
the thorn-crowned head of Jesus
through the glass.
I say Jesus because I followed
the red handprints on the brick
and there he was next door,
a bust in the window
of the botánica,
blood in his hair,
his eyes a bewildered blue
cast heavenward, hoping
for an airlift away from here.
The sign on the door
offered a manicure
with every palm reading.

DSS Dream

I dreamed
the Department of Social Services
came to the door and said:
"We understand
you have a baby,
a goat and a pig living here
in a two-room apartment.
This is illegal.
We have to take the baby away,
unless you eat the goat."

"The pig's OK?" I asked.
"The pig's OK," they said.

White Birch

for Katherine, December 28, 1991

Two decades ago rye whiskey
scalded your father's throat,
stinking from the mouth
as he stamped his shoe
in the groove between your hips,
dizzy flailing cartwheel down the stairs.
The tail of your spine split,
became a scraping hook.
For twenty years a fire raced
across the boughs of your bones,
his drunken mouth a movie
flashing with every stabbed gesture.

Now the white room of birth is throbbing:
the numbers palpitating red on the screen of machinery
tentacled to your arm; the oxygen mask wedged
in a wheeze on your face; the numbing medication
injected through the spine.
The boy was snagged on that spiraling bone.
Medical fingers prodded your raw pink center
while you stared at a horizon of water
no one else could see, creatures leaping silver
with tails that slashed the air
like your agonized tongue.

You were born in the river valley,
hard green checkerboard of farms,

a town of white birches
and a churchyard from the workhorse time,
weathered headstones naming women
drained of blood with infants coiled inside
the caging hips, hymns swaying
as if lanterns over the mounded earth.

Then the white birch of your bones,
resilient and yielding, yielded again,
root snapped as the boy spilled out of you
into hands burst open by beckoning
and voices pouring praise like water,
two beings tangled in exhaustion,
blood-painted, but full of breath.

After a generation of burning
the hook unfurled in your body,
the crack in the bone dissolved:
One day you stood, expected again
the branch of nerves
fanning across your back to flame,
and felt only the grace of birches.

The Other Alamo
San Antonio, Texas, 1990

In the Crockett Hotel dining room,
a chalk-faced man in medaled uniform
growls a prayer
at the head of the veterans' table.
Throughout the map of this saint-hungry city,
hands strain for the touch of shrines,
genuflection before cannon and memorial plaque,
grasping the talisman of bowie knife replica
at the souvenir shop, visitors
in white Biblical quote T-shirts.

The stones in the walls are smaller
than the fists of Texas martyrs;
their cavernous mouths could drink the canal to mud.
The Daughters of the Republic
print brochures dancing with Mexican demons,
Santa Anna's leg still hopping
to conjunto accordions.
The lawyers who conquered farmland
by scratching on parchment in an oil lamp haze,
the cotton growers who kept the time
of Mexican peasant lives dangling from their watchchains,
the vigilantes hooded like blind angels
hunting with torches for men the color of night,
gathering at church, the capitol, or the porch
for a century all said this: *Alamo.*

In 1949, three boys
in Air Force dress khaki
ignored the whites-only sign
at the diner by the bus station:
A soldier from Baltimore, who heard *nigger* sung here
more often than his name, but would not glance away;
another blond and solemn as his Tennessee of whitewashed spires;
another from distant Puerto Rico, cap tipped at an angle
in a country where brown skin
could be boiled for the leather of a vigilante's wallet.

The waitress squinted a glare and refused their contamination,
the manager lost his crewcut politeness
and blustered about local customs,
the police, with surrounding faces,
jeered about tacos and señoritas
on the Mexican side of town.
We're not leaving, they said,
and hunched at their stools
till the manager ordered the cook,
sweat-burnished Black man unable to hide his grin,
to slide cheeseburgers on plates
across the counter.
We're not hungry, they said,
and left a week's pay for the cook.
One was my father; his word for fury
is Texas.

This afternoon, the heat clouds the air like bothered gnats.
The lunch counter was wrecked for the dump years ago.
In the newspapers, a report of vandals
scarring the wooden doors
of the Alamo
in black streaks of fire.

The Skull Beneath the Skin of the Mango

El Salvador, 1992

The woman spoke
with the tranquillity of shock:
the Army massacre was here.
But there were no peasant corpses,
no white crosses; even the houses
gone. Cameras chattered,
notebooks filled with rows of words.
Some muttered that slaughter
is only superstition
in a land of new treaties and ballot boxes.

Everyone gathered mangoes
before leaving. An American reporter,
arms crowded with fruit, could not see
what he kicked jutting from the ground.
He glanced down and found his sneaker
pressing against the forehead
of a human skull, yellow
like the flesh of a mango.

He wondered how many skulls
are crated with the mangoes
for sale at market, how many
grow yellow flesh and green skin
in the wooden boxes exported
to the States. This would explain,

he said to me,
why so many bodies
are found without heads
in El Salvador.

When Songs Become Water

In January 1991, I had several poems published in *Diario Latino*, an opposition newspaper in El Salvador. In February 1991, *Diario Latino* was burned down, on the behalf and at the behest of the same forces the newspaper had opposed: the government, the military, the death squads. The newspaper rebuilt itself, publishing only a few pages a day, till eventually *Diario Latino* was back to full strength. In February, 1992, on the first anniversary of the fire, *Diario Latino* published the Spanish version of the following poem. The poem was written in response to the fire and in tribute to the courage of the people who run this newspaper, though the poem applies as well to any people anywhere in the world whose voices rise above the flames.

When Songs Become Water

for Diario Latino, *El Salvador,* 1991

Where dubbed commercials
sell the tobacco and alcohol
of a far winter metropolis,
where the lungs of night
cough artillery shots
into the ears of sleep,
where strikers with howls
stiff on their faces
and warnings pinned to their shirts
are harvested from garbage heaps,
where olive uniforms keep watch
over the plaza
from a nest of rifle eyes and sandbags,
where the government party
campaigns chanting through loudspeakers
that this country
will be the common grave of the reds,
there the newsprint of mutiny
is as medicine
on the fingertips,
and the beat of the press printing mutiny
is like the pounding of tortillas in the hands.

When the beat of the press
is like the pounding of tortillas,
and the newsprint is medicine

on the fingertips,
come the men with faces
wiped away by the hood,
who smother the mouth of witness night,
shaking the gasoline can across the floor,
then scattering in a dark orange eruption of windows,
leaving the paper to wrinkle gray in the heat.

Where the faces wiped away by the hood
are known by the breath of gasoline
on their clothes,
and paper wrinkles gray as the skin
of incarcerated talkers,
another Army helicopter plunges from the sky
with blades burning
like the wings of a gargoyle,
the tortilla and medicine words
are smuggled in shawls,
the newspapers are hoarded
like bundles of letters from the missing,
the poems become songs
and the songs become water
streaming through the arteries
of the earth, where others at the well
will cool the sweat in their hair
and begin to think.

V

from *Imagine the Angels of Bread* (1996)

Imagine the Angels of Bread

This is the year that squatters evict landlords,
gazing like admirals from the rail
of the roofdeck
or levitating hands in praise
of steam in the shower;
this is the year
that shawled refugees deport judges
who stare at the floor
and their swollen feet
as files are stamped
with their destination;
this is the year that police revolvers,
stove-hot, blister the fingers
of raging cops,
and nightsticks splinter
in their palms;
this is the year
that darkskinned men
lynched a century ago
return to sip coffee quietly
with the apologizing descendants
of their executioners.

This is the year that those
who swim the border's undertow
and shiver in boxcars
are greeted with trumpets and drums

at the first railroad crossing
on the other side;
this is the year that the hands
pulling tomatoes from the vine
uproot the deed to the earth that sprouts the vine,
the hands canning tomatoes
are named in the will
that owns the bedlam of the cannery;
this is the year that the eyes
stinging from the poison that purifies toilets
awaken at last to the sight
of a rooster-loud hillside,
pilgrimage of immigrant birth;
this is the year that cockroaches
become extinct, that no doctor
finds a roach embedded
in the ear of an infant;
this is the year that the food stamps
of adolescent mothers
are auctioned like gold doubloons,
and no coin is given to buy machetes
for the next bouquet of severed heads
in coffee plantation country.

If the abolition of slave-manacles
began as a vision of hands without manacles,
then this is the year;

if the shutdown of extermination camps
began as imagination of a land
without barbed wire or the crematorium,
then this is the year;
if every rebellion begins with the idea
that conquerors on horseback
are not many-legged gods, that they too drown
if plunged in the river,
then this is the year.

So may every humiliated mouth,
teeth like desecrated headstones,
fill with the angels of bread.

The Owl and the Lightning

Brooklyn, New York

No pets in the projects,
the lease said,
and the contraband salamanders
shriveled on my pillow overnight.
I remember a Siamese cat, surefooted
I was told, who slipped from a window ledge
and became a red bundle
bulging in the arms of a janitor.

This was the law on the night
the owl was arrested.
He landed on the top floor,
through the open window
of apartment 14-E across the hall,
a solemn white bird bending the curtain rod.
In the cackling glow of the television,
his head swiveled, his eyes black.
The cops were called, and threw a horse blanket
over the owl, a bundle kicking.

Soon after, lightning jabbed the building,
hit apartment 14-E, scattering bricks from the roof
like beads from a broken necklace.
The sky blasted white, detonation of thunder.
Ten years old at the window, I knew then that God
was not the man in my mother's holy magazines,
touching fingertips to dying foreheads

with the half-smile of an athlete signing autographs.
God must be an owl, electricity
coursing through the hollow bones,
a white wing brushing the building.

Cada puerco tiene su sábado

for Angel Guadalupe

Cada puerco tiene su sábado,
Guadalupe would say.
Every pig has his Saturday.

Guadalupe remembered a Saturday
in Puerto Rico, when his uncle Chungo
clanked a pipe across the skull of a shrieking pig,
wrestled the staggering blood-slick beast
before the flinching children.
Chungo set the carcass ablaze
to burn the bristles off the skin.
Guadalupe dreamt for years about
the flaming pig. Of his uncle,
he would only say:
Cada puerco tiene su sábado.
And Chungo died, diving into the ocean,
an artery bursting in his head.

I remember a Saturday
on Long Island,
when my father dug a pit
for the pig roast,
and neighbors spoke prophecy
of dark invasion
beneath the growl of lawnmowers.
I delivered the suckling pig,
thirty pounds in my arms,

cradled in a plastic bag
with trotters protruding
and flies bouncing off the snout,
skinned by a farmer
who did not know
the crunch of cuero.
My father cursed the lost skin,
cursed the rain filling the pit,
cursed the oven too small for the pig,
cursed the pig he beheaded
on the kitchen counter,
cursed his friends who left
before the pig was brown.

Amid the dented beer cans
leaning back to back,
I stayed with my cursing father.
I was his accomplice;
witnesses in doorways saw me
carrying the body through the streets.
I ate the pig too,
jaw grinding thick pork
like an outfielder's tobacco.
The farmer told me
the pig's name: Ichabod.

Cada puerco tiene su sábado.

The Piñata Painted with a Face Like Mine

I was in the basement when my brother came home
without a shirt covering his hungry chest.
He saw a fight by the river,
eight-track tapes stolen from somebody's car,
a broken bottle jammed in the armpit
and blood shooting out, so that even my brother's shirt
wrapped around the wound
did not keep the startled boy from dying.
That summer my brother stayed by the river,
passing the lukewarm wine or a pipe of hashish,
bragging about refrigerators of meat
plundered in unguarded garages.

I saw him slip the bills from my father's wallet
into his pants. When I told my brother this,
he promised a kitchen knife
plunged between my ribs as I slept.
Go get it, I said. When he turned
to the kitchen, a wave of blood crashed
in the chambers of my forehead.
Too quickly, my knuckles in his hair, his skull
thudding off the wall. I wanted to see
the blood irrigating the folds of his brain;
I wanted to break this piñata
painted with a face like mine.

Only amazement could have stopped me.
Amazing was the sight of my father's face.
He stood before us, a man with hands
forbidding as tarantulas, and cried.

After twenty years, one brother cannot sleep
waiting for the other. I wait for him,
the cool knife sliding against my skin.
And he waits for me, my knuckles in his hair,
to finish cracking open the piñata
painted with a face like mine.

Rednecks

Gaithersburg, Maryland

At Scot Gas, Darnestown Road,
the high school boys pumping gas
would snicker at the rednecks.
Every Saturday night there was Earl,
puckering his liquor-smashed face
to announce that he was driving
across the bridge, a bridge spanning
only the whiskey river
that bubbled in his stomach.
Earl's car, one side crumpled like his nose,
would circle slowly around the pumps,
turn signal winking relentlessly.

Another pickup truck morning,
and rednecks. Loitering
in our red uniforms, we watched
as a pickup rumbled through.
We expected: *Fill it with no-lead, boy,*
and gimme a cash ticket.
We expected the farmer with sideburns
and a pompadour.
We, with new diplomas framed
at home, never expected the woman.
Her face was a purple rubber mask
melting off her head, scars rippling down
where the fire seared her freak face,
leaving her a carnival where high school boys
paid a quarter to look, and look away.

No one took the pump. The farmer saw us standing
in our red uniforms, a regiment of illiterate conscripts.
Still watching us, he leaned across the seat of the truck
and kissed her. He kissed her
all over her happy ruined face, kissed her
as I pumped the gas and scraped the windshield
and measured the oil, he kept kissing her.

Do Not Put Dead Monkeys in the Freezer

Monkeys at the laboratory,
monkeys doing countless somersaults
in every cage on the row,
monkeys gobbling Purina Monkey Chow
or Fruit Loops with nervous greedy paws,
monkeys pressing faces
through a grille of steel,
monkeys beating the bars
and showing fang,
monkeys and pink skin
where fur once was,
monkeys with numbers and letters
on bare stomachs,
monkeys clamped and injected, monkeys.

I was a lab coat and rubber gloves
hulking between the cages.
I sprayed down the batter of monkeyshit
coating the bars, fed infant formula in a bottle
to creatures with real fingers,
tested digital thermometers greased
in their asses, and carried boxes of monkeys
to the next experiment.
We gathered the Fear Data, keeping score
as a mechanical head
with blinking red bulbs for eyes
and a siren for a voice

scared monkeys who spun in circles,
chattering instructions
from their bewildered brains.

I did not ask for explanations,
even when I saw the sign
taped to the refrigerator that read:
Do Not Put Dead Monkeys in the Freezer.
I imagined the doctor who ordered the sign,
the moment when the freezer door
swung open on that other face,
and his heart muscle chattered like a monkey.

So I understood
when a monkey leapt from the cage
and bit my thumb through the rubber glove,
leaving a dollop of blood that gleamed
like icing on a cookie.
And I understood when one day, the doctors gone,
a monkey outside the bell curve of the Fear Data
shrieked in revolt, charging
the red-eyed mechanical head
as all the lab coats cheered.

The Bouncer's Confession

I know about the Westerns
where stunt doubles bellyflop
through banisters rigged to collapse
or crash through chairs designed to splinter.
A few times the job was like that.
A bone fragment still floats
in my right ring finger
because the human skull
is harder than any fist.

Mostly, I stood watch at the door
and imagined their skulls
brimming with alcohol
like divers drowning in their own helmets.
Their heads would sag, shaking
to stay awake, elbows sliding out
across the bar.
I gathered their coats. I found their hats.
I rolled up their paper bags
full of sacred objects only I could see.
I interrogated them for an address,
a hometown. I called the cab,
I slung an arm across my shoulders
to walk them down the stairs.

One face still wakes me some mornings.
I remember black-frame eyeglasses

off-balance, his unwashed hair.
I remember the palsy that made claws
of his hands, that twisted his mouth
in the trembling parody of a kiss.
I remember the stack of books he read
beside the beer he would not stop drinking.
I remember his fainted face
pressed against the bar.
This time, I dragged a corkscrewed body
slowly down the stairs, hugged to my ribs,
his books in my other hand,
only to see the impatient taxi
pulling away. I yelled at acceleration smoke,
then fumbled the body with the books
back up the stairs, and called the cab again.

No movie barrooms. No tall stranger
shot the body spreadeagled across the broken table.
No hero, with a hero's uppercut, knocked them out,
not even me. I carried them out.

Soliloquy at Gunpoint
for José

I sat in the car,
window down in summer,
waiting. Two boys
from the neighborhood
peered in the car
and did not recognize me,
so one opened his gym bag
and flourished a revolver
with black tape on the handle,
brushing the barrel's tiny mouth
against my forehead.

I sat calm as a burning monk.
The only god in my meditation
was the one who splices the ribbon of film:
a screen full of gunmen with sleepwalker's gaze,
confident detectives in silk neckties,
the cooing of hostage negotiators,
soliloquy at gunpoint
recited without stuttering.

I spread my hand
as if to offer salt
to a licking dog.
The script said *Give me the gun,*
so I said *Give me the gun.*
And he did.

My Cockroach Lover

The summer I slept
on JC's couch,
there were roaches
between the bristles
of my toothbrush,
roaches pouring
from the speakers
of the stereo.
A light flipped on
in the kitchen at night
revealed a Republican
National Convention
of roaches,
an Indianapolis 500
of roaches.

One night I dreamed
a giant roach
leaned over me,
brushing my face
with kind antennae
and whispering *I love you.*
I awoke slapping myself
and watched the darkness
for hours, because I realized

this was a dream
and so that meant
the cockroach
did not really love me.

The Meaning of the Shovel

Barrio René Cisneros,
Managua, Nicaragua, June–July 1982

This was the dictator's land
before the revolution.
Now the dictator is exiled to necropolis,
his army brooding in camps on the border,
and the congregation of the landless
stipples the earth with a thousand shacks,
every weather-beaten carpenter
planting a fistful of nails.

Here I dig latrines. I dig because last week
I saw a funeral in the streets of Managua,
the coffin swaddled in a red and black flag,
hoisted by a procession so silent
that even their feet seemed
to leave no sound on the gravel.
He was eighteen, with the border patrol,
when a sharpshooter from the dictator's army
took aim at the back of his head.

I dig because yesterday
I saw four walls of photographs:
the faces of volunteers
in high school uniforms
who taught campesinos to read,
bringing an alphabet
sandwiched in notebooks
to places where the mist never rises

from the trees. All dead,
by malaria or the greedy river
or the dictator's army
swarming the illiterate villages
like a sky full of corn-plundering birds.

I dig because today, in this barrio
without plumbing, I saw a woman
wearing a yellow dress
climb into a barrel of water
to wash herself and the dress
at the same time,
her cupped hands spilling.

I dig because today I stopped digging
to drink an orange soda. In a country
with no glass, the boy kept the treasured bottle
and poured the liquid into a plastic bag
full of ice, then poked a hole with a straw.

I dig because today my shovel
struck a clay bowl centuries old,
the art of ancient fingers
moist with this same earth,
perfect but for one crack in the lip.

I dig because I have hauled garbage
and pumped gas and cut paper
and sold encyclopedias door to door.
I dig, digging until the passport
in my back pocket saturates with dirt,
because here I work for nothing
and for everything.

Thieves of Light

Chelsea, Massachusetts, 1991

We all knew about Gus:
the locksmith, the Edison man, and me.
We heard about the welfare hotel,
where he stacked clothes
on the sidewalk for the garbage truck
if no rent was paid by Wednesday morning.
We heard about the triple-deckers,
where he heaved
someone else's chair or television
from the third floor, and raged
like a drunk blaming his woman
till the pleading tenant agreed to leave.
There was word he even shot a cop
twenty years ago, but the jury
knew Gus too, studying cuticles
or the courtroom clock
as the foreman said not guilty.
The only constable in Chelsea
wore his gun in a shoulder holster,
drooped his cigarette at a dangerous angle,
yet claimed that Gus
could not be found on Broadway
to serve a summons in his hand.

This is how we knew Gus:
Luisa saw the sludge plop
from the faucet, the mice

dropping from the ceiling,
shook her head and said no rent,
still said no after his fist
buckled the bolted door.
In the basement, Gus hit switches.
The electric arteries in the walls
stopped pumping, stove cold,
heat off, lightbulbs gray.
She lived three months in darkness,
the wax from her candle spreading
over the kitchen table like a calendar
of the constant night,
sleeping in her coat, a beggar
in the underworld kingdom of rodents.
When Luisa came to me, a lawyer
who knew Spanish,
she kept coughing
into her fist, apologizing
with every cough.

So three strangers
gathered in the hallway.
The locksmith
kneeled before the knob
on the basement door,
because I asked him
to be a burglar today.

The Edison man swallowed dryly,
because I asked him
to smuggle electricity today,
forget Gus's promise
of crushed fingers.
And me: the lawyer, tightly
rolling a court order in my hand
like a newspaper to swing at flies,
so far from the leatherbound books
of law school, the treatises
on the constitution
of some other country.

We worked quickly, thieves of light.
The door popped open,
as in a dream of welcome,
swaying with the locksmith's fingers.
The Edison man pressed his palms
against the fuse boxes
and awakened the sleeping wires
in the walls. I kept watch by the door,
then crept upstairs, past Gus's office
where shadows and voices
drove the blood in my wrist
still faster. I tapped on Luisa's door.
I had to see if the light was on.

She stared at me
as if the rosary
had brought me here
with this sudden glow from the ceiling,
a stove where rice and beans
could simmer, sleep without a coat.
I know there were no angels
swimming in that dim yellow globe,
but there was a light louder than Gus,
so much light
I had to close my eyes.

Offerings to an Ulcerated God

Chelsea, Massachusetts

Mrs. López refuses to pay rent,
and we want her out,
the landlord's lawyer said,
tugging at his law school ring.
The judge called for an interpreter,
but all the interpreters were gone,
trafficking in Spanish
at the criminal session
on the second floor.

A volunteer stood up in the gallery.
Mrs. López showed the interpreter
a poker hand of snapshots,
the rat curled in a glue trap
next to the refrigerator,
the water frozen in the toilet,
a door without a doorknob.
(No rent for this. I know the law
and I want to speak,
she whispered to the interpreter.)

Tell her she has to pay
and she has ten days to get out,
the judge commanded, rose
so the rest of the courtroom rose,
and left the bench. Suddenly
the courtroom clattered

142

with the end of business:
the clerk of the court
gathered her files
and the bailiff went to lunch.
Mrs. López stood before the bench,
still holding up her fan of snapshots
like an offering this ulcerated god
refused to taste,
while the interpreter
felt the burning
bubble in his throat
as he slowly turned to face her.

My Native Costume

When you come to visit,
said a teacher
from the suburban school,
don't forget to wear
your native costume.

But I'm a lawyer,
I said.
My native costume
is a pinstriped suit.

You know, the teacher said,
a Puerto Rican costume.

Like a guayabera? The shirt? I said.
But it's February.

The children want to see
a native costume,
the teacher said.

So I went
to the suburban school,
embroidered guayabera
short-sleeved shirt
over a turtleneck,
and said, Look kids,
cultural adaptation.

Her Toolbox

for Katherine Gilbert-Espada,
Boston, Massachusetts

The city was new, so new
that she once bought
a set of knives
from the trunk of a car
and saw them rust
after the first rinsing.
She gathered with the tourists
at the marketplace of city souvenirs.
Still, she was the carpenter
for the community center
on Dorchester Avenue,
where men with baseball bats
chased the new immigrants
and even the liberals
rolled up their windows
at a red light.

The car on Dorchester Avenue
trailed behind her one night
as she walked to the subway.
The man talked to her
while he steered, kept taunting
when the car lurched
onto the sidewalk,
trapping her in a triangle
of brick and fender.
He knew her chest was throbbing;

that was the reason he throbbed too,
stepping from the car.

But the carpenter
unlocked her toolbox
and raised a hammer up
as if a nail protruded
from between his eyebrows,
ready to spike his balsawood forehead.
Oh, the hands like startled pigeons
flying across his face
as he backpedaled to the car
and rolled his window shut.

After the rusting discount knives,
the costly city souvenirs,
the men who gripped the bat
or the steering wheel
to keep from trembling,
she swung her toolbox walking
down Dorchester Avenue.

When the Leather is a Whip

At night,
with my wife
sitting on the bed,
I turn from her
to unbuckle
my belt
so she won't see
her father
unbuckling
his belt

Because Clemente Means Merciful

for Clemente Gilbert-Espada,
February 1992

At three A.M., we watched
the emergency room doctor
press a thumb against your cheekbone
to bleach your eye with light.
The spinal fluid was clear, drained
from the hole in your back,
but the X-ray film
grew a stain on the lung,
explained the seizing cough,
the wailing heat of fever:
pneumonia at the age
of six weeks, a bedside vigil.
Your mother slept beside you,
the stitches of birth still burning.

When I asked, *Will he be OK?*
no one would answer: *Yes.*
I closed my eyes and dreamed
my father dead, naked on a steel table
as I turned away. In the dream,
when I looked again,
my father had become my son.

So the hospital kept us: the oxygen mask,
a frayed wire taped to your toe
for reading the blood,
the medication forgotten from shift to shift,

a doctor bickering with radiology over the film,
the bald girl with a cancerous rib removed,
the pediatrician who never called, the yawning intern,
the hospital roommate's father
from Guatemala, ignored by the doctors
as if he had picked their morning coffee,
the check marks and initals at five A.M.,
the pages of forms flipping like a deck of cards,
recordkeeping for the records office,
the lawyers and the morgue.

One day, while the laundry
in the basement hissed white sheets,
and sheets of paper documented dwindling breath,
you spat mucus, gulped air, and lived.
We listened to the bassoon of your lungs,
the cadenza of the next century, resonate.
The Guatemalan father
did not need a stethoscope to hear
the breathing, and he grinned.
I grinned too, and because Clemente
means merciful, stood beside the Guatemalteco,
repeating in Spanish everything
that was not said to him.

I know someday you'll stand beside
the Guatemalan fathers,

speak in the tongue
of all the shunned faces,
breathe in a music
we have never heard, and live
by the meaning of your name.

The Prisoners of Saint Lawrence

Riverview Correctional Facility,
Ogdensburg, New York, 1993

Snow astonishing their hammered faces,
the prisoners of Saint Lawrence, island men,
remember in Spanish the island places.

The Saint Lawrence River churns white into Canada, races
past barbed walls. Immigrants from a dark sea find oceanic
snow astonishing. Their hammered faces

harden in city jails and courthouses, indigent cases
telling translators, public defenders what they
remember in Spanish. The island places,

banana leaf and nervous chickens, graces
gone in this amnesia of snow, stinging cocaine
snow, astonishing their hammered faces.

There is snow in the silence of the visiting room, spaces
like snow in the paper of their poems and letters, that
remember in Spanish the island places.

So the law speaks of cocaine, grams and traces,
as the prisoners of Saint Lawrence, island men,
snow astonishing their hammered faces,
remember in Spanish the island places.

All the People Who are Now Red Trees

When I see the red maple,
I think of a shoemaker
and a fish peddler
red as the leaves,
electrocuted by the state
of Massachusetts.

When I see the red maple,
I think of flamboyán's red flower,
two poets like flamboyán
chained at the wrist
for visions of San Juan Bay
without Navy gunboats.

When I see the flamboyán,
I think of my grandmother
and her name, Catalán for red,
a war in Spain
and nameless laborers
marching with broken rifles.

When I see my grandmother
and her name, Catalán for red,
I think of union organizers
in graves without headstones,
feeding the roots
of red trees.

When I stand on a mountain,
I can see the red trees of a century,
I think red leaves are the hands
of condemned anarchists, red flowers
the eyes and mouths of poets in chains,
red wreaths in the treetops to remember,

I see them raising branches
like broken rifles, all the people
who are now red trees.

Sleeping on the Bus

How we drift in the twilight of bus stations,
how we shrink in overcoats as we sit,
how we wait for the loudspeaker
to tell us when the bus is leaving,
how we bang on soda machines
for lost silver, how bewildered we are
at the vision of our own faces
in white-lit bathroom mirrors.

How we forget the bus stations of Alabama,
Birmingham to Montgomery,
how the Freedom Riders were abandoned
to the beckoning mob, how afterward
their faces were tender and lopsided as spoiled fruit,
fingers searching the mouth for lost teeth,
and how the riders, descendants
of Africa and Europe both, kept riding
even as the mob with pleading hands wept fiercely
for the ancient laws of segregation.

How we forget Biloxi, Mississippi, a decade before,
where no witnesses spoke to cameras,
how a brown man in military uniform
was pulled from the bus by police
when he sneered at the custom of the back seat,
how the magistrate proclaimed a week in jail
and went back to bed with a shot of whiskey,

how the brownskinned soldier could not sleep
as he listened for the prowling of his jailers,
the muttering and cardplaying of the hangmen
they might become.
His name is not in the index;
he did not tell his family for years.
How he told me, and still I forget.

How we doze upright on buses,
how the night overtakes us
in the babble of headphones,
how the singing and clapping
of another generation
fade like distant radio
as we ride, forehead
heavy on the window,
how we sleep, how we sleep.

The Fugitive Poets of Fenway Park

Boston, Massachusetts, 1948

The Chilean secret police
searched everywhere
for the poet Neruda: in the dark shafts
of mines, in the boxcars of railroad yards,
in the sewers of Santiago.
The government intended to confiscate his mouth
and extract the poems one by one like bad teeth.
But the mines and boxcars and sewers were empty.

I know where he was.
Neruda was at Fenway Park,
burly and bearded in a flat black cap, hidden
in the kaleidoscope of the bleachers.
He sat quietly, chomping a hot dog
when Ted Williams walked to the crest of the diamond,
slender as my father remembers him,
squinting at the pitcher, bat swaying in a memory of trees.

The stroke was a pendulum of long muscle and wood,
Ted's face tilted up, the home run
zooming into the right field grandstand.
Then the crowd stood together, cheering
for this blasphemer of newsprint, the heretic
who would not tip his cap as he toed home plate
or grin like a war hero at the sportswriters
surrounding his locker for a quote.

The fugitive poet could not keep silent,
standing on his seat to declaim the ode
erupted in crowd-bewildering Spanish from his mouth:

Praise Ted Williams, raising his sword
cut from the ash tree, the ball
a white planet glowing in the atmosphere
of the right field grandstand!

Praise the Wall rising
like a great green wave
from the green sea of the outfield!

Praise the hot dog, pink meat,
pork snouts, sawdust, mouse feces,
human hair, plugging our intestines,
yet baptized joyfully with mustard!

Praise the wobbling drunk, seasick beer
in hand, staring at the number on his ticket,
demanding my seat!

Everyone gawked at the man standing
on his seat, bellowing poetry in Spanish.
Anonymous no longer,
Neruda saw the Chilean secret police
as they scrambled through the bleachers,

pointing and shouting, so the poet
jumped a guardrail to disappear
through a Fenway tunnel,
the black cap flying from his head
and spinning into center field.

This is true. I was there at Fenway
on August 7, 1948, even if I was born
exactly nine years later
when my father
almost named me Theodore.

Hands Without Irons Become Dragonflies

Clemente Soto Vélez (1905–1993) was a great Puerto Rican poet and political figure. He was an important activist in the Nationalist Party, a militant organization fighting for the independence of Puerto Rico and led by Pedro Albizu Campos. Soto Vélez participated in a Nationalist assault on the capitol building in 1932. He was also editor of a Party newspaper called *Armas* (Weapons). Charged with seditious conspiracy, he was imprisoned from 1936 to 1940, briefly released, then imprisoned again until 1942. Following his release in 1942, he settled in New York, where he again worked as a journalist, and was a key organizer in East Harlem for Congressman Vito Marcantonio and the American Labor Party. He was recognized as a major poet with the publication of *Caballo de palo* (The Wooden Horse) in 1959; verses from that book are quoted, in translation, in the twelfth stanza ("You spelled your name Klemente with a K"). Soto Vélez would serve as mentor to countless writers and artists in New York's Puerto Rican community.

He was also my friend. My wife and I named our son after him. We introduced the two Klementes on Columbus Day, 1992. Clemente Soto Vélez died in April, 1993, and was buried in Lares, the town of his birth, which was also the site of a historic 1868 uprising against the Spanish. The following elegy was spurred by a visit to his grave in 1994.

Hands Without Irons Become Dragonflies

for Clemente Soto Vélez
Born 1905, Lares, Puerto Rico
Died 1993, Santurce, Puerto Rico

Hands without irons become dragonflies,
red flowers rain on our hats,
subversive angels flutter like pigeons from a rooftop,
this stripped and starving earth is not a grave.

Clemente, listen to the history
before your birth. Lares, 1868:
the leaves drooping like elephant ears,
the coffee whirling gently as the danza
of unperspiring linen and lace,
the boots clicking across the plaza for church
and the hour fanning the face of the clock on the steeple,
the bar in the mouth of a straining horse
and the dark man choked with a collar of spikes
for slipping chains and fleeing into the river:
all as coins in the palm of a distant king,
all the inventory of Spain.

One night after sleep in September,
the merchants fumbled
with wire spectacles at the window
to witness the levitation of rebel machetes.
The mayor curled on the floor of his own jail,
peasants showered in wine
looted from forbidden cellars,
and slaves marveled as hands without irons
became dragonflies.

Soon the Spanish troops
would sweep through Lares
dragging the cannon's operatic mouth,
and the rebels died from yellow fever
in prison, the loudly humming darkness
of Aguadilla.

When you were born, Clemente,
beneath the vigilance of midwife mountains,
the merchants of sugar and tobacco in this country
spoke with Yankee accents; the soldiers
bellowed in English and stared at what they wanted.
Their language by law
condemned the handcuffed in the courthouse,
confusing stoic children in schoolrooms of wood.
The Protestant governor promised toilets,
sucked the sugar from the stalk, then
orchestrated flags and choirs for the battleship landing
of Theodore Roosevelt.
The President scribbled notes about the flora
and snorted at the barefoot crowds.

Your people were peasants without soil,
buried in the soil
while their hair was still black.
But in the plaza of Lares,
the muttering of fever-mad revolutionaries

brushed across your neck,
pausing in the hollow of your ear.
The ancianos, with skin like cured tobacco leaves,
remembered 1868,
taught you in hoarse conspiracy
that a machete could chop
the wrist of a landlord
easily as cane.

Hands without irons become dragonflies,
red flowers rain on our hats,
subversive angels flutter like pigeons from a rooftop,
this stripped and starving earth is not a grave.

In San Juan, his eye measuring
the imperious white pillars,
a poet from Lares
appeared at the crest of the crowd
pounding sixteen hundred hands
against the doors of the capitol building.
A sergeant insisted on his weight
before you. Then an unknown hand,
a hand of the sixteen hundred hands
gripped yours and left a pearl-handled revolver
in your grasp. Your aim, inches
from the sergeant's mouth,
created in him a guard dog

quivering at the cry of thunder,
created in you a poetry like ammunition.
All night you halted the cars passing
through the old city, leaning in windows
with a burnished gun,
demanding a shout of *Viva Puerto Rico Libre*,
payment better than paper dollars
with their portraits of kings called Presidents.
Those years, like water
plunging from an anvil-headed mountain:
Albizu in eulogy held the ashes of cremated insurgents
to the sky, and the radio banned his trembling staccato,
so you committed alchemy with ink and paper in the half-light,
words black as the sleeping shoes of laborers.

Meditations on the jailhouse ceiling:
La Princesa's crumbling skin
in the summer of accusation,
the printer in his apron
nodding to police
and newspapers confiscated in bundles.
This is the law of poets and their newspapers:
for the word *weapons*, a cell with no toilet;
for the word *revolution*, a door bolted in rust;
for the word *Yankee*, a window blindfolded with bars;
for the words *Puerto Rico*, a wall of cockroaches
too fat to kill with a fist.

Your poems became a crust
sealing your eyelids, a wet string of coughing
in your throat. In Ponce, police fired bullets
through the palms of toppling demonstrators.

After four years walking clockwise in the prison yard,
after one month on parole, the courtroom
was the chapel where a heretic was ordered to pray.
The hearing was in English. The judge was thinking, in English,
about the August temperatures in Puerto Rico
and the ceiling fan flailing overhead.
The defendant Soto Vélez learned
about Lucky Strikes and Karl Marx in prison,
but forgot which words were forbidden by parole.
Four speeches in four towns, throat raw
as a swallow of smoke from shouting.
Two more years' incarceration.
The judge remembered a photograph
from thirty years ago, Theodore Roosevelt
in a white suit and Panama hat
driving a steam shovel through the canal.
The judge did not realize then
how easily the linen wrinkles,
how the heat brings palpitations.

Hands without irons become dragonflies,
red flowers rain on our hats,

subversive angels flutter like pigeons from a rooftop,
this stripped and starving earth is not a grave.

East Harlem after the War:
the ward heelers blustered
that the Red Congressman
bought steamship tickets and welfare
for every Puerto Rican coming to East Harlem,
so they would mark their ballots with his name:
Vito Marcantonio, American Labor Party.
The ward heelers never heard you at the microphone,
Clemente, your American Labor Spanish
spreading in the sky like a flamboyán tree
split through cement, till the immigrants in the street
swore red flowers rained on their hats
and floated in the shovels of their hands.
Back in San Juan, the mayor ordered snow at Christmas
dumped on the city parks
by a squadron of bombers.

You spelled your name Klemente with a K,
conjured a new alphabet
so no one kept from school could misspell a word.
Your poems were subversive angels
born in the sky,
an insurrection of sunflowers,
a goddess of fireflies,

a hurricane of persecuted stars,
a river rising on your lover's tongue.
When children drowned in the fires
of tenement wiring,
or poets burned their intestines with alcohol
to collapse on some deserted beach
of East Harlem sidewalk, you sang the poems
till your hands cramped in their fists.

Hands without irons become dragonflies,
red flowers rain on our hats,
subversive angels flutter like pigeons from a rooftop,
this stripped and starving earth is not a grave.

The first time we saw you,
you leaned over a sick woman
in bed. You loosened the bow tie
looping your neck, pushed your sleeves
back to the elbow
and pressed two fingers,
dry and delicate as straw,
against the swollen streams
in her head, sapped the storm raining there.
We could see the lightning branch
in the blue veins behind your knuckles,
and imagined the manacles
snapped across each wrist, as if

the blockade of blood to your fingers
could asphyxiate the brain.
Later, you spoke of Puerto Rico
with an exile's music:
fluorescent creatures in the water,
the caves like great eyelids of mist,
the pulp scraped from a mango seed.

The last time we saw you,
your hair was white ash against the pillow,
though we told ourselves this was not the white
of a murdered forest, but white anemone
floating, white coral sprouting
from your forehead.
You touched the face of my infant son,
named after you, as you would touch
a lost photograph,
the book where it was hidden
many years ago.
You fed us all the communion of praise,
eyes still black and bright as volcanic glass,
though the work of breathing
exhausted you to sleep.
So you slept, mouth agape,
wheezing through bloated lungs, your hands
laced across your stomach.
We knew your hands were closing,

prayed for open palms
fluttering those subversive angels to the sky
like pigeons from a rooftop.

Hands without irons become dragonflies,
red flowers rain on our hats,
subversive angels flutter like pigeons from a rooftop,
this stripped and starving earth is not a grave.

Klemente, today we visit your island grave.
We light a candle for you in chapel
beneath a Christ executed with beggar's ribs
and knees lacerated red.
He is a Puerto Rican Christ.
In San Juan Bay, a tanker from New Jersey
bursts a black artery bubbling to the surface,
so troops along the beach
in sanitary metallic suits
scoop the oil clotted into countless bags
while helicopters scavenge from above.
Lares now is the property of the state:
the tamarindo tree
planted for independence
in the plaza
blotched and gray, a rag
tied around one branch
like a tourniquet.

At the Lares cemetery nearly a year ago,
your box sank into a hole
brimming with rainwater.
Today the grave we find is desolate clay,
parched and cracking, a plank marked M75.
He is here: burial mound 75, says the gravedigger.
So the poet who named us
suffocates in the anonymity of dirt.
This is how the bodies of dissenters disappear,
beneath oceans coated with tankers' blood,
down to the caves where their voices still drip,
as the authorities guarantee
that this stripped and starving earth is not a grave,
and no one pays the man who carves the stone.
We bury a book with you, pry red flowers
from the trees to embroider the ground,
negotiate the price and labor for a gravestone
as the child with your name races between the tombs.

Klemente, you must be more
than the fragile web of handkerchief
you left behind.
You claimed your true age
was ten thousand light-years,
promised that you would someday explode
in atoms, showering down
on us in particles beyond the spectrum

of our sight, visible only to the deities
carved into the boulders by original people
slaughtered five centuries ago.
Now a dragonfly drifts to the forehead
of a vagabond declaiming groggy rebellion
in the plaza, insect-intoxicated,
protesting his own days blindfolded with bars,
his faith louder than an infected mouth.
He says that he remembers you.
On the road to Lares, a horse without a rope
stands before the cars in glowering silence,
infuriating traffic, refusing to turn away
his enormous head. We know
what the drivers must do to pass:
shout *Viva Puerto Rico Libre.*

Hands without irons become dragonflies,
red flowers rain on our hats,
subversive angels flutter like pigeons from a rooftop,
this stripped and starving earth is not a grave.

VI

from *A Mayan Astronomer in Hell's Kitchen* (2000)

My Name is Espada

Espada: the word for sword in Spain
wrought by fire and the hammer's chime,
name for the warrior reeling helmet-hooded
through the pandemonium of horses in mud,
or the face dreaming on a sarcophagus,
hands folded across the hilt of stone.

Espada: sword in el Caribe,
rapier tested sharp across the bellies of Indios, steel tongue
lapping blood like a mastiff gorged on a runaway slave,
god gleaming brighter than the god nailed to the cross,
forged at the anvil with chains by the millions
tangled and red as the entrails of demons.

Espada: baptizing Taíno or Congolese,
name they stuttered in the barking language
of priests and overseers, slave's finger pressed to the blade
with the pulsing revelation that a Spaniard's throat
could seep blood like a fingertip, sabers for the uprising
smuggled in the hay, slave of the upraised saber
beheaded even as the servants and field hands
murmured he is not dead, he rides a white horse at night,
his sword is a torch, the master cannot sleep,
there is a dagger under the pillow.

Espada: cousin to the machete, peasant cutlass
splitting the cane like a peasant's backbone,

cousin to the kitchen knife skinning a plátano.
Swords at rest, the machetero or cook
studied their blisters as if planets
to glimpse the hands of their father the horseman,
map the hands of their mother the serf.

Espada: sword in Puerto Rico, family name of bricklayers
who swore their trowels fell as leaves from iron trees;
teachers who wrote poems in galloping calligraphy;
saintcarvers who whittled a slave's gaze and a conqueror's beard;
shoemaker spitting tuberculosis, madwoman
dangling a lantern to listen for the cough;
gambler in a straw hat inhabited by mathematical angels;
preacher who first heard the savior's voice
bleeding through the plaster of the jailhouse;
dreadlocked sculptor stunned by visions of birds,
sprouting wings from his forehead, earthen wings in the fire.

So the face dreaming on a sarcophagus,
the slave of the saber riding a white horse by night
breathe my name, tell me to taste my name: Espada.

The Shiny Aluminum of God

Carolina, Puerto Rico, 1997

After the pilgrimage
to the Office of Cemetery Records,
we pay fifty dollars in cash
for the free municipal burial plot,
the clerk hiding the bills in a manila folder.
El pastor Pentecostal forgets the name of the dead,
points at the ceiling and gazes up
whenever he loudly whispers the syllables
for eternal life, *la vida eterna,*
as if the stain on the tile were the map of heaven.
The mourners are palm trees in the hallelujah wind,
hands raised overhead. Once grandmother Tata's pen
looped the words of the spirits as they spoke to her;
now she grips a borrowed golden crucifix
in the coffin, lid propped open by mistake.
The coffin bumps into a hole of mud
next to the chain-link fence, and then
the family Vélez Espada gathers for dinner.

The pernil is frozen, pork shoulder congealed and raw
like a hunk of Siberian woolly mammoth.
But Angela tells us of the miracle pot
that will roast the meat in an hour
without a cup of water. She sells the pot
to her neighbors too, keeps a tower of boxes
with a picture of the pot resplendent on every box.
The words on her kerchief hail
the shiny aluminum of God: *Dios te ama.*

The scar carves her husband's forehead
where the doctors scooped the tumor out,
where cancer cells scramble like a fistful of ants.
In a year he will be the next funeral, when the saints
of oncology surrender their weapons. For now
Edwin lives by the finches he snares in the backyard,
wings blundering through the trap door of the cage,
sold for five dollars apiece to the neighbors.
He praises God for brain surgery and finches,
leans close and grins about the time
his brother somersaulted out a window
and two swooping angels caught him
by the elbows, inches from the ground.
Only one broken rib, Edwin says,
rubbing his stomach in the slow way
of a man satisfied with his meal.
Angela's brother passes out pamphlets:
God's ambulance found him and his needle
in a condemned building, no shoes
and no heartbeat. Then Edwin says:
God will not let me die.

An hour later,
the pernil is still frozen in the oven.
Angela stares at the sweating pork,
then the boxes of pots unsold in the corner.

A boy cousin taps his fork
and asks if we can eat the finches.
The trap clatters in the backyard,
an angel flapping in the cage.

My Father as a Guitar

The cardiologist prescribed
a new medication
and lectured my father
that he had to stop working.
And my father said: *I can't.*
The landlord won't let me.
The heart pills are dice
in my father's hand,
gambler who needs cash
by the first of the month.

On the night his mother died
in faraway Puerto Rico,
my father lurched upright in bed,
heart hammering
like the fist of a man at the door
with an eviction notice.
Minutes later,
the telephone sputtered
with news of the dead.

Sometimes I dream
my father is a guitar,
with a hole in his chest
where the music throbs
between my fingers.

For the Jim Crow Mexican Restaurant in Cambridge, Massachusetts, Where My Cousin Esteban was Forbidden to Wait Tables Because He Wears Dreadlocks

I have noticed that the hostess in peasant dress,
the wait staff and the boss
share the complexion of a flour tortilla.
I have spooked the servers at my table
by trilling the word *burrito*.
I am aware of your T-shirt solidarity
with the refugees of the Américas,
since they steam in your kitchen.
I know my cousin Esteban the sculptor
rolled tortillas in your kitchen with the fingertips
of ancestral Puerto Rican cigarmakers.
I understand he wanted to be a waiter,
but you proclaimed his black dreadlocks unclean,
so he hissed in Spanish
and his apron collapsed on the floor.

May La Migra handcuff the wait staff
as suspected illegal aliens from Canada;
may a hundred mice dive from the oven
like diminutive leaping dolphins
during your Board of Health inspection;
may the kitchen workers strike, sitting
with folded hands as enchiladas blacken
and twisters of smoke panic the customers;
may a Zapatista squadron comandeer the refrigerator,
liberating a pillar of tortillas at gunpoint;
may you hallucinate dreadlocks

braided in thick vines around your ankles;
and may the Aztec gods pinned like butterflies
to the menu wait for you in the parking lot
at midnight, demanding that you spell their names.

Pegao

We Puerto Ricans say
that the hard rice
stuck to the bottom
of the pot
is a delicacy.
We scrape
with the spoon
like kitchen archaeologists.

Maybe it's the cost of rice.
Maybe we see the rice
stuck to the bottom
of the pot
as a metaphor.
Or maybe
we have learned to chew
the ow in pegao.

A Mayan Astronomer in Hell's Kitchen

9th Avenue and West 48th Street, New York,
October 1998

Above the deli in Hell's Kitchen where the fire erupted,
above the firefighters charging with hoses like great serpents,
above the fingerprints of smoke smearing the night,
above the crowd calling his name with tilted faces,
above the fire truck and its ladder reaching for him,

a man leaned elbows on the third-floor fire escape,
bronze skin, black hair in a braid, leather jacket,
with a grin for the firefighters
bellowing at the crowds to *stand back*,
a Mayan astronomer in Hell's Kitchen
watching galaxies spiral in the fingerprints of smoke,
smoking a cigarette.

The Community College Revises its Curriculum in Response to Changing Demographics

SPA 100 Conversational Spanish
2 credits

The course
is especially concerned
with giving police
the ability
to express themselves
tersely
in matters of interest
to them

The Death of Carmen Miranda

Dying on television,
on *The Jimmy Durante Show*,
spinning another samba for the tourists
when she staggered beneath the banana headdress
and dropped to one knee.
The audience began to giggle
at the wobbly pyramid of bananas,
but the comedian with the fat nose and the fedora
growled *Stop the music!* and lifted her up.
I cannot find my breath, Carmen said,
fingers fanning across her chest.
The mouth of the camera opened
to chuckle at her accent, but then
widened into an astonished *Oh*.

Later that night, at the mansion,
her maid found Carmen sleeping without breath,
could not unlock the mirror from her fingers.
The hair no one saw on television was unpinned,
grown long beneath the banana headdress,
bleached yellow like the bananas.

Genuflection in Right Field

We played hardball
in a triangle of grass by the highway ramp.
The outfield was dangerous:
the ball hopping off the roof of a car,
driver leaning big-fisted from the window
like a furious newscaster
bursting through the television screen.
Once a boy we knew
from the neighborhood
circled us, whirling a chain overhead.
We left him sobbing in the grass
after the chain slapped his knees.

One afternoon, we found a pit in right field.
A dog curled dead at the bottom,
fur charred in clumps, a stake jammed
in the split eye socket. We told each other
we had seen this before: the human corpse
bleeding through white plastic garbage bags
and dumped on the hill not far away.
We swore we heard that body moan,
and named the place Dead Man's Hill,
police tape holding us back
like the red velvet rope of a museum.

But the dog was here. We took our positions
with the ceremonial pounding of fist into glove.

The smart hitters poked the ball into right field,
knowing that not one of us could chase it
without pausing at the grave
to glimpse the snarl of a putrified snout,
a fumbling genuflection, the wobbly throw,
the hooting of obscenities from the infield.

Prisoner AM-8335 and His Library of Lions

for Mumia Abu-Jamal
SCI-Greene, Waynesburg, Pennsylvania,
May 2, 1998

When the guards handcuffed inmates in the shower
and shoved them skidding naked to concrete,
or the blueshirts billyclubbed a prisoner
to wrench the gold from his jaw,
to swirl KKK in his spat blood,
the numbered men pressed their fingertips
against the smooth cool pages of your voice,
that voice of many books,
and together you whispered in the yard
about lawsuits, about the newspapers.

From the battlements
the warden trumpeted a proclamation:
in every cell one box per inmate,
twelve by twelve by fourteen,
for all personal possessions. You say
four blueshirts crowded your death row cell
to wrestle seventeen cartons away,
wrinkled paperbacks in pillars
toppling, history or law collected and studied
like the bones of a fossilized predator,
a library beyond Carnegie's whitest visions of marble.
One guard would fondle a book emblazoned
with the word *Revolutionary*, muttering:
this is what we're supposed to get.

Today, after the hunger strike,
you sit windowed in the visiting room,
prisoner AM-8335: dreadlocks blooming
like an undiscovered plant of the rain forest,
hands coupled in the steel cuffs,
brown skin against the striped prison jumpsuit,
tapestry of the chain gang.

I would rather be beaten, you say,
than this assault on the life of the mind.
You keep Toni Morrison's book in your box with the toothpaste.
You stare through the glass at the towering apparition
of your library, as if climbing marble steps.

And you say:
Giving up a book is like giving up a child,
like parting with your own flesh.
How do you choose between Beloved
and The Wretched of the Earth.

Your eyes pool.
A single tear is the scarification of your cheekbone,
a warrior's ceremonial gash on death row.
Across the glass a reflection of the guards walking,
small blue men patrolling your forehead.

In the parking lot, I turn again towards the prison,
walls ribboned with jagged silver loops of wire,
and see a great library
with statues of lions at the gate.

Compañero Poet and the Surveillance of Sheep

for Andrew Salkey, 1928–1995
Amherst, Massachusetts

Your redbrick house is surrounded by sheep.
They pucker their snouts against the wire fence
and watch for you to slide the window open.
They refuse to believe your coffin has flown
like baggage to England.

Now a college bureaucrat sleeps in your house.
The sheep copulate for the college farm program.
Years ago, we noticed the surveillance of sheep,
loudly said they must be FBI. One day,
an agent will sneeze, his nose clogged
with hay and wool, another shorn with clippers
as he wails about his secret work.
The sheep have never read you, but reports
of your subversion nip their ears, relentless as mites.

Poet, you saw Chile from the window of that house:
the perspiration glimmering in the pouches
beneath the eyes of a weary torturer;
the last note trembling on the E string of a guitar
stripped from the hands of an executed singer;
yet also saw the dark grain in the photographs
of the disappeared, the placard aloft in the plaza;
saw that smoke from the charred books and rooftops
always evaporates in a sky ancient with human fumes.

Teacher, you saw Jamaica from the doorway of that house:
the blood under the right thumbnail of your ancestor
cutting the cane for English tea, Jamaican rum;
the scabbed roads of bullwhip across the ribs,
the head on a pike stabbed in the left ear by crows;
yet also saw the musket blast of the Maroon,
rebel slave stuffing powder and lead into the barrel
as redcoated soldiers bled with astonished eyebrows;
saw maternal cheekbones in the mango fattened
and dropped from the tree, envisioned adolescence
in a wooden fishing boat cradled by the flash of the Caribbean Sea.

Diabetes was your chupacabras, the bloodsucker.
Feet amputated, you hopped without toes.
Your fingers twined around the crook of your cane,
the hands consoling each other
for the loss of their brother feet.
Still, you cackled as I ate too many roasted potatoes
from your table. You wrote an ode to orange chicken;
forbidden ginger ice cream, you tasted the words,
sharp and cold.

The sheep cannot believe the accounts of your death, the ambulance
stumbling too late across craters on the road to the hospital.
The sheep wait for the moment to stampede your library,
chew your books, peer through your window and door.
But because of you, poet, teacher, the sheep must watch me

and everyone who ever gazed at the monument of your bookshelves.
or prayed for the nova in your poems to flood the mountains.
The sheep are staring yet.

Your beard still sprouts from my jaw. Because of you,
Chile is a bird pressed flat in my book, Jamaica
a brown hand gathering stones on the beach
for snapping at the noses of gargantuan conquerors.
For you, I savor the burst of air
in the word *compañero.*

I Apologize for Giving You Poison Ivy by Smacking You in the Eye with the Crayfish at the End of My Fishing Line

for Katherine

I apologize for not knowing how to fish.
In Brooklyn all the fish are dead,
from the goldfish spinning in the toilet bowl
to the bluefish on ice at the market
with eyes like Republicans campaigning for Congress.
Once my brother and I went fishing on a lake.
We argued about who was rowing wrong
for half an hour, until we discovered
that the boat was still chained to the dock.

I apologize for not knowing poison ivy.
In my neighborhood everything was poisoned,
the silver clouded water from the tap
and the rainbow gasoline puddle at the curb.
The bricklayer inside my body
stacked the bricks of pollution row by row, so now
if I eat fresh vegetables I might have a stroke.
But I can sit for hours in a patch of poison ivy
without a single welt, head bobbing
as Joe Cuba yells *bang-bang* in the headphones.

(I apologize to the crayfish impaled on my hook.
I am a killer with fogged vision and a tremor in my hands.
I was told that if I went fishing I would relax
and my hands would stop shaking, so the crayfish,
cockroach of the lake, became the panicky bait.
In Puerto Rico the cockroaches

are bigger than this crayfish and they fly,
and no one uses them for bait.)

I apologize for tangling my fishing line in the poison ivy
and whipping it free at the moment
you approached me with an offering of lemonade.
I apologize for the hooked crayfish, oiled with poison ivy,
that flew over my shoulder like a cockroach with wings
and smacked you in the eye.

I apologize for the way your eye ballooned
so you resembled a middleweight
the referee would rescue against the ropes.
I apologize for the splotches that erupted
in scarlet fireworks across your face.
I apologize for the emergency room.
I apologize for the bills from the hospital
that pile like a snowdrift against the mailbox;
when the credit agency calls,
I tell the man that I have a gun
and I know where he works.

I have decided on my penance.
I will return to the lake at midnight
in my swim trunks, and stand there
with arms spread stiff
like a scarecrow beckoning mosquitoes,

and as they milk my veins
I will shout this poem repeatedly
till sunrise, or until the police
club me with their flashlights.

Thanksgiving

This was the first Thanksgiving with my wife's family,
sitting at the stained pine table in the dining room.
The wood stove coughed during her mother's prayer:
Amen and the gravy boat bobbing over fresh linen.
Her father stared into the mashed potatoes
and saw a white battleship floating in the gravy.
Still staring at the mashed potatoes, he began a soliloquy
about the new Navy missiles fired across miles of ocean,
how they could jump into the smokestack of a battleship.
"Now in Korea," he said, "I was a gunner and the people there
ate kimch'i, and it really stinks." Mother complained that no one
was eating the creamed onions. *"Eat, Daddy."* The creamed onions
look like eyeballs, I thought, and then said, "I wish I had missiles
like that." Daddy laughed a 1950's horror-movie mad-scientist laugh,
and told me he didn't have a missile, but he had his own cannon.
"Daddy, eat the candied yams," Mother hissed, as if he were
a liquored CIA spy telling secrets about military hardware
to some Puerto Rican janitor he met in a bar. "I'm a toolmaker.
I made the cannon myself," he announced, and left the table.
"Daddy's family has been here in the Connecticut Valley since 1680,"
Mother said. "There were Indians here once, but they left."
When I started dating her daughter, Mother called me a half-Black,
but now she spooned candied yams on my plate. I nibbled
at the candied yams. I remembered my own Thanksgivings
in the Bronx, turkey with arroz y habichuelas and plátanos,
and countless cousins swaying to bugalú on the record player
or roaring at my grandmother's Spanish punchlines in the kitchen,

the glowing of her cigarette like a firefly lost in the city. For years
I thought everyone ate rice and beans with turkey at Thanksgiving.
Daddy returned to the table with a cannon, steering the black
steel barrel. "Does that cannon go boom?" I asked. "I fire it
in the backyard at the tombstones," he said. "That cemetery bought
up all our farmland during the Depression. Now we only have
the house." He stared and said nothing, then glanced up suddenly,
like a ghost had tickled his ear. "Want to see me fire it?" he grinned.
"Daddy, fire the cannon after dessert," Mother said. "If I fire
the cannon, I have to take out the cannonballs first," he told me.
He tilted the cannon downward, and cannonballs dropped
from the barrel, thudding on the floor and rolling across
the brown braided rug. Grandmother praised the turkey's thighs,
said she would bring leftovers home to feed her Congo Gray parrot.
I walked with Daddy to the backyard, past the bullet holes
in the door and his pickup truck with the Confederate license plate.
He swiveled the cannon around to face the tombstones
on the other side of the backyard fence. "This way, if I hit anybody,
they're already dead," he declared. He stuffed half a charge
of gunpowder into the cannon, and lit the fuse. From the dining room,
Mother yelled, *"Daddy, no!"* Then the battlefield rumbled
under my feet. My head thundered. Smoke drifted over
the tombstones. Daddy laughed. And I thought: When the first
drunken Pilgrim dragged out the cannon at the first Thanksgiving—
that's when the Indians left.

The River Will Not Testify

Connecticut River
Turners Falls, Massachusetts, 1999

The river's belly swirls shards of bone gnawed by water.
The river is deaf after centuries of pummeling the rocks.
The river thrashes all night with the lightning of lunatic visions.
The river strangles on the dam, hissing at the stone eagles
that watch with stone eyes from the bridge.
Concrete stops the river's tongue at Turners Falls.

The river cannot testify to all the names:
Peskeomskut, gathering place at the falls;
Sokoki, Nipmuck, Pocumtuck, many nations, many hands
that speared the flapping salmon from the rocks,
stitched the strips of white birch into wigwams.
So Reverend Mr. Russell wrote to the Council of War:
They dwell at the Falls a considerable number, yet
most of them old men, women and children. The Lord calls us
to make some trial which may be done against them.

The river cannot testify of May 19, 1676.
The river's face was painted blue at daybreak.
Captain Turner's men, Puritans sniffing with beards
and flintlock muzzles, slipped between the wigwams
ghostly as the smoke from drying fish.
Their muskets lifted up the flaps of bark;
their furious God roared from every musket's mouth.
The sleepers drenched in rivers sun-red like the salmon,
and a wailing rose with the mist from the skin of the river.

The river cannot testify about canoes skidding
over the falls, their ribs in splinters, or swimmers
hammering their skulls against the rocks,
or bullets hammering the rocks and skulls,
or Captain Holyoke's sword lopping the branches
of grandfathers into the water, or Bardwell
counting the corpses vomited by the white cascade.
And Reverend Mr. Mather wrote:
The river swept them away, that ancient river, oh my soul.

The river cannot testify to who began the rumor:
a thousand Indians, someone yelled, a thousand Indians approaching;
so when a few dozen warriors read the smoke from gutted wigwams
and splashed across the river, the conquerors fled,
shrieking at the green demons that whipped their eyes
and snatched their ankles as they stumbled through the forest.

The river cannot testify to say what warrior's musket
shot Captain Turner, the ball of lead thudding
between shoulder blades, flipped from his horse
and dragged off by the water to sink in a halo of blood.
His name christened the falls, the town, the granite monument
that says: *destroyed three hundred Indians at this place.*
One day a fisherman would unearth shinbones
of Indians by the falls, seven skeletons
and each one seven feet tall, he declared.

Centuries gone, the fishing boats sucked over the dam,
the tendons of the bridge ripped out in the flood,
the children leaning too far and abducted by the current:
all as withered leaves to the river.
The lumber company fire that smothered the night watchman,
the cotton mill and the needles of brown lung,
the knife factory bricked shut during the Depression:
all mosquito-hum and glimmer of porchlight to the river.
The Horse Thief Detecting Society that never caught a thief,
the German Military Band flourishing trombones,
the Order of Scalpers with fraternity war whoops,
the American Legion dinners beery against communism,
the Indians galloping undefeated onto the high school football field:
all like the glitter of fish to the river.

Centuries from now, at this place,
when chimneys are the shadows of monsters in the river,
when collapsed spires are haunted by crows,
when graves are plowed to harvest the bones
for aphrodisiacs and trinkets,
when the monuments of war have cracked
into hierogylphics no one can read,
when the rain sizzles with a nameless poison,
when the current drunk on its own dark liquor
storms through the crumbling of the dam,
the river will not testify of Turners Falls,
for the river has swept them away, oh my soul.

VII

Alabanza: New Poems (2002)

En la calle San Sebastián

Viejo San Juan, Puerto Rico, 1998

Here in a bar on the street of the saint
en la calle San Sebastián,
a dancer in white with a red red scarf
en la calle San Sebastián,
calls to the gods who were freed by slaves
en la calle San Sebastián,
and his bronze face is a lantern of sweat
en la calle San Sebastián,
and hands smack congas like flies in the field
en la calle San Sebastián,
and remember the beat of packing crates
en la calle San Sebastián,
from the days when overseers banished the drum
en la calle San Sebastián,
and trumpets screech like parrots of gold
en la calle San Sebastián,
trumpets that herald the end of the war
en la calle San Sebastián,
as soldiers toss rifles on cobblestone
en la calle San Sebastián,
and the saint himself snaps an arrow in half
en la calle San Sebastián,
then lost grandfathers and fathers appear
en la calle San Sebastián,
fingers tugging my steel-wool beard
en la calle San Sebastián,

whispering *your beard is gray*
en la calle San Sebastián,
spilling their rum across the table
en la calle San Sebastián,
till cousins lead them away to bed
en la calle San Sebastián,
and the dancer in white with a face of bronze
en la calle San Sebastián,
shakes rain from his hair like the god of storms
en la calle San Sebastián,
and sings for the blood that drums in the chest
en la calle San Sebastián,
and praises the blood that beats in the hands
en la calle San Sebastián,
en la calle San Sebastián.

Now the Dead Will Dance the Mambo
Achill Island, Ireland, June 2000

Last night the shadow of a cloud rolled off the bare mountain
like a shawl slipping from the shoulder of a giant.
Shirts on the clothesline sagged in rain.
We burned turf, fists of earth blackening in the fireplace,
room full of poets' books leaning rumpled, half-asleep.
All night a radio sang in Irish, tongues sod-hard with lament
or celebration. Then the BBC news, and the announcer's lips
pinching the name: *Tito Puente, The Mambo King, dead in New York.*

I would listen to Tito's records and see my father years ago:
black hair shiny as the spinning disk, combed slick
before the dance. I learned to spy on his mambo step,
drummed the pots and kitchen tables of Brooklyn.
I saw Tito Puente too, hammering timbales on the Jazzboat
in Boston Harbor, brandishing drumsticks overhead
to scatter the malevolent spirits that grabbed at his hair.
Guadalupe pushed backstage to return with Tito's drumstick,
splintered from repeating, always repeating the beat of slaves.
Here, on this island, I rehearse the Irish word for drum:
bodhrán, gripped by hand like the pandereta,
circle of skin and wood for the grandchildren of slaves
to thump as they sang the news in Ponce, Puerto Rico.

Again today the rain grays the graying stones.
We shake away drizzle in the pub dwarfed by mountains.
In brown Guinness light we squint to see

the posters of their Easter dead: James Connolly
bellowing insurrection to the Citizen Army,
the year *1916* ablaze above his head, numbers torched
like the pillars of an empire's monuments to itself.
The bartender says Connolly eyed the firing squad
strapped to a chair in the stonebreakers' yard,
gangrene feasting on his wound so he could not stand.
I tell the bartender that Puerto Rico has its Easter dead:
a march on Palm Sunday, colonial police intoxicated
by the incense of gunsmoke, Cadets of the Republic
painting slogans on the street in their belly-blood.
That was Ponce in 1937, and Rafael still says:
My mother left in a white dress and came home in a red dress.

Tito Puente is dead, and we are in a pub on Achill Island
plundering the jukebox, flipping between the Wolfe Tones
and the Dubliners till we discover Tito's *Oye Como Va.*
The beat is a hand slapping the bar, heads nodding
as if their ears funneled a chant of *yes-yes, yes-yes,*
and when we shoot a game of pool in his memory
the table becomes a dance floor at the Palladium,
cue ball spinning through a crowd of red and green.
Now James Connolly could dance the mambo,
gangrene forever banished from his leg.

Contemplation

for Tommy Patten (1910–1936)
Achill Island, Ireland

You told your brother:
The bullet that will get me
won't get a Spanish worker,
so the bullet got you,
for Madrid, the Spanish Republic, all workers
says your black memorial stone, yes,

but also for a white house on Dooega Bay,
solitary as a white boat at sea,
the village asleep in wings of slate,
the mountain listening to the tide with a foggy head;

and time enough so anyone
—your thirteen brothers and sisters,
the boys pale like you at the Guinness factory,
the poet born here who returns with a white beard—
could sit on this hill beside your black stone
to contemplate the mountain, the village,
the white house, the bay at Dooega.

Offering of Stones

Deserted Village, Achill Island, Ireland, May 2000

Your house greets a stranger with an offering of stones:
round stones like the eggs of a great gray bird,
flat stones the sandals of a giant, hearth stones
awaiting the next ember, gable stones that muscled the missing roof,
ledge-stones where you once curled asleep with straw.
For a mile the collar of stone studs the mountain's throat:
columns stacked for doorways by hands with Neolithic ancestors
entombed on the next hill, windows in slits where you shivered
as if the battering raindrops were volleys of British lead,
mounds of walls fallen useless as potatoes with blight
or peasants without rent, nearly a hundred houses gone to stone,
naked against the wind cantering down the slope with a bluster of
      battlecries.
Yet I am welcome to the hearth and kettle for the story you must tell,
so I squat between the nettles and grass sprouting from the floor to
      listen.

First came the fungus, mush and stink of potatoes
in the hole, then the faces cliff-gaunt or boulder-swollen,
riot of lice in the rags, dysentery's lava, delirium
or teeth spat free by scurvy, rapping on the door and no one there,
famine dead without coffins rolled into the sand
at the shoreline. Sir Richard and his bailiffs evicted the living,
hauled off the roof and confiscated the kettle so none could return.
Some walked to the shore, scavenging for seaweed and eels;
others staggered across the decks of ships bound for America,
where the steel in cauldrons boiled for them as if brewing the fever,

where the loom clacked like a skeleton dancing at the wake,
where servants labored in a stone mansion by the sea
as the master quill-penned poetry, until they slept on shelves
in a room at the top of the stairs, hanging from the wall
because potato rot birthed servants in Ireland, country of rain
that would never dampen their skin again.

Now in your village there is sheep dung fertilizing the rock.
Two child-shepherds, brother and sister, chase their flock
into the ruins, between the jagged walls smoking with fog,
through doorways standing alone in the rubble's ebb,
widows who gazed at the sea till they became stone.
One sheep has escaped, kneeling at the graves
of three drowned fishermen in the churchyard down below.
There is no dog to steer the lambs, so the girl yaps and trills.
To climb I grip the ledge of rock and find the cool of your dying hand,
and I would lift your head so you could see the shepherds
outrun by the flock, glimpse the ocean's skirt,
tell me of the pirate queen, her castle at Kildavnet.

Sheep Haiku

Achill Island, Ireland

A lone sheep cries out:
There are more of us than them!
The flock keeps grazing.

Circle Your Name

for Camilo Pérez-Bustillo
Ciudad de México, March 1996

Fingered: Two Hundred Enemies of the System
says the headline in *Excelsior,*
and your name is on the list
of subversives counted by the state,
your name a strand
in the black braid of names on the page,
because the bus drivers on strike
need your lawyer's words to translate
the echo of their empty mouths,
because union leaders watch their shadows
leak and stain the jailhouse walls
as you tap messages to the human rights office,
because you have seen the masked comandantes
in the mountains, and have sworn to them
that we will know of every peasant grave
shoveled by soldiers, where many fingertips
poke through soil like new shoots of grass.

So I fax my letter to Amnesty International
and the Mexican Consulate in Boston
as if the litany of your name
will string an amulet around your neck,
remembering the judge
who refused to sign an order arresting the strikers,
his skull bullet-burst like the lightbulb
dropped today on the floor of my kitchen.
So I tell you never to walk alone,

change your route to work, slip away
from every new hand pressing your shoulder
and calling you compañero, and in your *yes*
I hear you will forget, squeezing onto the same bus
every morning to sweat with all the others
who sweat on buses, their skin brilliant.
And I want to say: *Leave México.*
I promise you bookstores in Boston.
There is Szechuan chicken at the Yenching,
subversion of your tongue in the red peppers.

Years ago, after the coup,
there came reports from Estadio Chile
about the man in a hood striding beside police
down the line of chill-drenched prisoners,
saying with a finger: *Him. Her. Him.*
If his neighbors ever learn his name,
the man in the hood will moan for clemency
from his wheelchair.

Unfold the newspaper hidden in your desk.
Circle your name as the informer did.
Frame the headline and the black braid of names;
dangle the frame from a crooked nail.
The marble general on horseback in the plaza
will rear up, his mustache bristling with jealousy

at your unwanted prize, and the police
will forget your face, gaping at dreams
of Jesus leaping from the cross to strangle them in bed,
his thorns scraping the howl in their cheekbones.

Searching for La Revolución
in the Streets of Tijuana
for Leroy Quintana

We began by driving across the border into México,
searching for a burrito with *mole* sauce
that would stir the celibate tongue of a saint.
A border patrol van snored on the first hill
like a watchdog dreaming of meat.
We parked the car and walked through Tijuana.

My guide was Nuevo Mexicano, who thirty years before
did reconnaissance for the Army in Vietnam.
Once I saw a python curling down
from a branch over my head, he said,
and his finger snaked the air
as if the python still startled him every night.

We saw no pythons in Tijuana,
but two men streaked by leading a white burro
painted with black stripes, costumed as a zebra.
A limousine bounced down the avenue,
the groom in a white tuxedo sprouting like a lily
from the open roof as everyone cheered.
We wandered through streets named for Villa and Zapata,
a bookstore with parchment-light yellowing the window.
A fraternity at Yale boasts the skull of Pancho Villa
in a glass case, leaving skulls of sugar in Tijuana.

Undressing tamales steamed in the husk,
we remembered parking at the corner

of La Revolución and La Constitución,
two avenues that never intersect.
So we walked among the herds
of beer-loud college boys from San Diego,
stripjoint shills testifying to glory
like Jesus had returned as a woman sliding naked down a pole,
beggars in traffic shedding their fingerprints
to blossom in a field of shut windows,
traders kneeling on blankets with clay gods
dwarfed and sightless in our hands.

At every corner
we stopped to gnaw on roasted corn
and ask the peddler:
¿Dónde está La Revolución?
And every peddler of roasted corn
waved and said: *Más allá.*
Far from here. Keep walking.

Sing Zapatista

March 6, 2001
Tepoztlán, State of Morelos, México

Sing the word *Tepoztlán*, Place of Copper,
pueblo of cobblestone and purple blossoms
amid the cliffs, serpent god ablaze with plumage
peering from the shaven rock.

Sing the word *Zapata*, bandoliers crossing his chest
like railroad tracks about to explode, rebellion's black iris
in 1910, in his eye the peasants of Morelos husking rifles
stalk by stalk from the cornfields.

Sing the word *Zapatista*, masked rebels riding now
in a caravan without rifles, tracking the long rosary of blood
beaded and stippled across the earth by other rebels the color of earth,
bus panting uphill saddled with ghosts dangling legs from the roof.

Sing the words *Félix Serdán*, age eleven when he straddled the horse
to ride with Zapata, witness to a century's harvest of campesino skulls
abundant as melons, twined in white mustache and blanket
beside the comandantes on the platform.

Sing the word *comandante*, twenty-three of the faceless
masked in black so their brown skin could grow eyes and mouths,
smuggling Mayan tongues to the microphone in the plaza
where the church drowses in dreams of Latin by rote.

Sing the word *durito*, hard little one, scarab on a banner
draped across the face of the church where bells bang

to welcome the rebels, as the scarab-people cluster below
shouting their vow never to be crushed by the shoe.

Sing the word *zapateado*, tap and stamp of women dancing in the plaza
to the hummingbird rhythms of Veracruz, guitarist in fedora
watching his fingers skitter like scarabs across the wood,
shawled dancer lost in the percussion of her feet.

Sing the word *Marcos*, el Subcomandante, and listen
when he says above the crowd chanting his name:
Marcos does not exist. I am a window. I am a mirror.
I am you. You are me.

Ezequiel

for Ezequiel Hernández, 1979–1997
Redford, Texas

Ezequiel, boy with the name of a prophet,
prodding your goats after school through the brush on the border,
you cannot know what bullet's detonation rained blood
from the tree of your aorta, who the sharpshooter was
that gripped the M-16 and drilled a shot between your ribs
from seven hundred feet away, why the Marines
camouflaged in leaves, faces painted brown,
did not radio for an ambulance when they stepped over you
sprawled across the dry well at twilight.

Ezequiel, they were hunting for smugglers of marijuana
who creep across the border costumed as herdsmen,
so they tracked you and the goats for twenty minutes
through the arroyo. They claim you raised your grandfather's .22,
kept for spooking packs of dogs, and fired with a smuggler's eye,
though the compass of your body in death pointed away from them,
the bullet's map scrutinized by headshaking investigators.
Ezequiel, your father heard the shot that killed you
from his cinderblock house, and his fingertips were shocked
by the current of his own blood leaking into the sand.

Ezequiel, a grand jury refused to indict the Marines.
These are warriors who decapitate the armies of skeletons
clattering across the border at the command of Mexican druglords.
Now that a white cross blooms like a cactus from your skull,
no one will hear your prophecy. No one knows that you saw
the Marines in visions: each with skin of burnished copper,

each with four wings and four faces, lion, bull, eagle, man, rising
in a whirlwind from the north, as they handed a torch between them
and lightning shot from the flame. Ezequiel, the roaring in your ears
was the drumroll of wings, the helicopter lifting your corpse.
The wheel you dreamed in the sky was the circle of a chopper blade.

Ezequiel, you have seen their holy city
with smoke gushing from every window;
you have seen their rivers boil.
Their sentries watch the desert, listening for the shriek
of tattooed tribesmen, shooting at the clank of a goat's bell.
Meanwhile the priests hoard warheads and uranium bullets
in the temple. The weapons' skin will blaze with fever,
pestilence glowing molten red in the mouths of aristocrats
who fling their gold into the streets.
When the city walls collapse, the teeth of slaves
will glint like seashells embedded in the stone.
Ezequiel, you would warn them,
but the bullet petrified your oracle's tongue.

Ezequiel, you are buried in the valley of dry bones.
There is thirst in the wood of your white cross,
heat in the tire planted with sunflowers by your grave,
prophecy in the bones. When your voice booms
over the desert, all the bones will rise knocking,
skulls snapping hard onto spines, sinew roping around shoulders,

flesh swelling like bread on sinew, and the four winds
gusting breath into the lungs of the dead. Ezequiel,
you will walk again with your grandfather of the .22 rifle.
You will walk again with your goats.

Parole Hearing

After three hours of interrogation by the parole board,
and the prisoner repeating *I did not do this thing*,
his brown hands were trembling, and the trembling
spilled his plastic cup at the table
where the prisoner sat, and his body stiffened
as the water oozed across the table to the edge,
inches from the prisoner's lap and his blue suit,
and the seven faces of the parole board
watched the puddle creeping closer,
and their silence was the silence of water
half a mile down, till one of them asked
You need something to wipe that up?
as if to say *You will die in prison*,
and the prisoner, his breath returned,
raised his head and answered *Yes*,
as if to say *I did not do this thing*.

How I Became the Rare *Iguana Delicatissima* of the Caribbean

The flypaper at the pet store dangled six feet
from the floor, four inches too low for me.
I was staring at the iguana, wondering
if he really was savory as a drumstick,
when I backed into the glue strip
that coiled and coiled around my head.
Dead flies stuck to my hair and shirt
like raisins dipped in honey;
I charged down the aisle
chanting the word *bathroom*,
dragging the manager away
from his sleepy ferrets.

In the bathroom I scrubbed my molting skin
and foamed my hair into spikes.
I glanced up to see myself in the mirror
with the bulging eyes of an iguana,
1950's science fiction movie dinosaur
that gobbled cavemen like gingerbread cookies,
and like the rare *Iguana delicatissima* of the Caribbean
I yearned for a rain forest cloudburst
to rinse my scaly neck,
but there was only the manager
apologizing with a coupon
for pet food anywhere in the store.
I want freeze-dried worms, I hissed. *And flies.*

The Monsters at the Edge of the World
for my wife Katherine

The film of your brain
is a map drawn by conquerors
flying the banner of exploration
and misnaming all the islands,
yet we sail through the clouds
swirling in this hemisphere,
navigate rivers of silver
till we find the white slash
circled in red that tells us
stroke, hemorrhage,
as if saying that monsters dwell here
at the edge of the world, and nowhere
do we see the lake where one night
we drifted in a wooden boat
with a bottle of wine
and dangled sparklers
over the starry water.

Inheritance of Waterfalls and Sharks

for my son Klemente

In 1898, with the infantry from Illinois,
the boy who would become the poet Sandburg
rowed his captain's Saint Bernard ashore
at Guánica, and watched as the captain
lobbed cubes of steak at the canine snout.
The troops speared mangos with bayonets
like many suns thudding with shredded yellow flesh
to earth. General Miles, who chained Geronimo
for the photograph in sepia of the last renegade,
promised Puerto Rico the *blessings of enlightened civilization.*
Private Sandburg marched, peeking at a book
nested in his palm for the words of Shakespeare.

Dazed in blue wool and sunstroke, they stumbled up the mountain
to Utuado, learned the war was over, and stumbled away.
Sandburg never met great-great-grand uncle Don Luis,
who wore a linen suit that would not wrinkle,
read with baritone clarity scenes from *Hamlet*
house to house for meals of rice and beans,
the Danish prince and his soliloquy—*ser o no ser*—
saluted by rum, the ghost of Hamlet's father wandering
through the ceremonial ballcourts of the Taíno.

In Caguas or Cayey Don Luis
was the reader at the cigar factory,
newspapers in the morning,
Cervantes or Marx in the afternoon,
rocking with the whirl of an unseen sword

when Quijote roared his challenge to giants,
weaving the tendrils of his beard when he spoke
of labor and capital, as the tabaqueros
rolled leaves of tobacco to smolder in distant mouths.

Maybe he was the man of the same name
who published a sonnet in the magazine of browning leaves
from the year of the Great War and the cigar strike.
He disappeared; there were rumors of Brazil,
inciting canecutters or marrying the patrón's daughter,
maybe both, but always the reader, whipping Quijote's sword overhead.

Another century, and still the warships scavenge
Puerto Rico's beaches with wet snouts. For practice,
Navy guns hail shells coated with uranium over Vieques
like a boy spinning his first curveball;
to the fisherman on the shore, the lung is a net
and the tumor is a creature with his own face, gasping.

This family has no will, no house, no farm, no island.
But today the great-great-great-grand nephew of Don Luis,
not yet ten, named for a jailed poet and fathered by another poet,
in a church of the Puritan colony called Massachusetts,
wobbles on a crate and grabs the podium
to read his poem about El Yunque waterfalls
and Achill basking sharks, and shouts:
I love this.

The Poet in the Box
for Brandon

We have a problem with Brandon,
the assistant warden said.
He's a poet.

At the juvenile detention center
demonic poetry fired Brandon's fist
into the forehead of another inmate.
Metaphor, that cackling spirit, drove him to flip
another boy's cafeteria tray onto the floor.
The staccato chorus rhyming in his head
told him to spit and curse
at enemies bigger by a hundred pounds.
The gnawing in his rib cage was a craving for discipline.
Repeatedly two guards shuffled him
to the cell called the box, solitary confinement,
masonry of silence fingered by hallucinating drifters,
rebels awaiting execution, monks in prayer.

Then we figured it out, the assistant warden said.
He started fights so we'd throw him
in solitary, where he could write.

The box: There poetry was a grasshopper in the bowl of his hands,
pencil chiseling letters across his notebook
like the script of a pharaoh's deeds on pyramid walls;
metaphor spilled from the light he trapped
in his eyelids, lamps of incandescent words;
rhyme harmonized through the voices

of great-grandmothers and sharecropper bluesmen
whenever sleep began to whistle in his breath.
So the cold was a blanket to him.

We fixed Brandon, the assistant warden said.
We stopped punishing him. He knows
that every violation means he stays here longer.

Tonight there are poets
who versify vacations in Tuscany,
the villa on a hill, the light of morning;
poets who stare at computer screens
and imagine cockroach powder
dissolved into the coffee
of the committee that said no to tenure;
poets who drain whiskey bottles
and urinate on the shoes of their disciples;
poets who cannot sleep as they contemplate
the extinction of iambic pentameter;
poets who watch the sky, waiting for a poem
to plunge in a white streak through blackness.

Brandon dreams of punishment,
stealing the keys from a sleepy jailer
to lock himself into the box, where he can hear
the scratching of his pencil
like fingernails on dungeon stone.

The Matchbook-Poet and His Scintilla of Fire

for Jonathan Klate
and Ozzy Klate (1977–1994)

When I tell you that I knew your son,
that I remember his eyes
huge behind wire spectacles,
investigator's eyes enormous from years
searching through the magnifying glass,

when I recall his poems
stacked by the hundreds in notebooks
the way he piled white dishes in the kitchen
at the diner where I met him,

I see your face become a field
and all the seasons flashing there,
fogged and clearing and fogged again,
blaze of sunlight through the grass
or blaze of ice across the earth,

which is how you tell me
about the morning you shook him
and he did not roll or yawn,
and the poem he left scratched into a matchbook,

and I know you light a cigarette
as you bend over the grave,
hands offering up this scintilla of fire,
so I would load your hands with poems and poems
he wrote today on the bus or at the diner,

my black ink cracking through the white:
write another poem,
write another poem,
your father is waiting.

Ghazal for Open Hands

in memory of Agha Shahid Ali
December 10, 2001
Northampton, Massachusetts

The imam stands above your grave to pray with open hands,
cupping your spirit like grain in the palms of these open hands.

Poet of Kashmir, the graveyard lathers my shoes with mud
as the imam calls to Islam's God and lifts his open hands.

Ghazal-maker, your pine box sinks into a cumulus of snow,
red earth thumping on the coffin, dropped from open hands.

There are some today who murmur of the cancer in your brain
but do not know the words for speaking to Allah with open hands.

We listen to Islamic prayers at the cemetery, as we pay for bombs
to blossom into graves in places where they pray with open hands.

Far from here, the bombs we bless are tumbling down in loaves
of steel to tear away the fingers from their hungry open hands.

Shahid, your grave multiplies wild as cancer cells across Afghani earth,
countless prayers reverberating in the well of the throat, in open hands.

I cannot scrape off the mud choking my shoes or blink away the vision
of reaching into the hole for you, my hands open to your open hands.

Alabanza: In Praise of Local 100

*for the 43 members of Hotel Employees and Restaurant Employees
Local 100, working at the Windows on the World restaurant,
who lost their lives in the attack on the World Trade Center*

Alabanza. Praise the cook with a shaven head
and a tattoo on his shoulder that said *Oye,*
a blue-eyed Puerto Rican with people from Fajardo,
the harbor of pirates centuries ago.
Praise the lighthouse in Fajardo, candle
glimmering white to worship the dark saint of the sea.
Alabanza. Praise the cook's yellow Pirates cap
worn in the name of Roberto Clemente, his plane
that flamed into the ocean loaded with cans for Nicaragua,
for all the mouths chewing the ash of earthquakes.
Alabanza. Praise the kitchen radio, dial clicked
even before the dial on the oven, so that music and Spanish
rose before bread. Praise the bread. *Alabanza.*

Praise Manhattan from a hundred and seven flights up,
like Atlantis glimpsed through the windows of an ancient aquarium.
Praise the great windows where immigrants from the kitchen
could squint and almost see their world, hear the chant of nations:
Ecuador, México, Republica Dominicana,
Haiti, Yemen, Ghana, Bangladesh.
Alabanza. Praise the kitchen in the morning,
where the gas burned blue on every stove
and exhaust fans fired their diminutive propellers,
hands cracked eggs with quick thumbs
or sliced open cartons to build an altar of cans.
Alabanza. Praise the busboy's music, the *chime-chime*
of his dishes and silverware in the tub.

Alabanza. Praise the dish-dog, the dishwasher
who worked that morning because another dishwasher
could not stop coughing, or because he needed overtime
to pile the sacks of rice and beans for a family
floating away on some Caribbean island plagued by frogs.
Alabanza. Praise the waitress who heard the radio in the kitchen
and sang to herself about a man gone. *Alabanza.*

After the thunder wilder than thunder,
after the shudder deep in the glass of the great windows,
after the radio stopped singing like a tree full of terrified frogs,
after night burst the dam of day and flooded the kitchen,
for a time the stoves glowed in darkness like the lighthouse in Fajardo,
like a cook's soul. Soul I say, even if the dead cannot tell us
about the bristles of God's beard because God has no face,
soul I say, to name the smoke-beings flung in constellations
across the night sky of this city and cities to come.
Alabanza I say, even if God has no face.

Alabanza. When the war began, from Manhattan and Kabul
two constellations of smoke rose and drifted to each other,
mingling in icy air, and one said with an Afghan tongue:
Teach me to dance. We have no music here.
And the other said with a Spanish tongue:
I will teach you. Music is all we have.

GLOSSARY

Alabanza Praise; sometimes used in a religious sense. From "alabar," to celebrate with words.

Albizu Campos, Pedro Leader of the pro-independence Nationalist Party in Puerto Rico, who was imprisoned with Clemente Soto Vélez and others in 1936, convicted of seditious conspiracy. A Harvard lawyer, Albizu spent most of three decades incarcerated.

American Labor Party Left-wing, union-based political party of the 1930s through the 1950s.

anciano Elderly person.

arroz y (or **con**) **habichuelas** Rice and beans.

barrio Latino neighborhood.

Barrio René Cisneros Community constructed in Managua, Nicaragua, after the Sandinista Revolution on land expropriated from the Somoza dynasty; named for a combatant killed in that revolution.

bodhrán Handheld drum used in Ireland.

Borinquen Corruption of the original indigenous name for the island of Puerto Rico, "Boriken."

botánica Syncretic religious shop, specializing in spiritism, full of herbs, potions, statues, books, etc.

bugalú Latin music popular in New York during the mid-1960s, combining rhythm-and-blues with traditional Cuban elements and bilingual (Spanish-English) lyrics.

caciques Leaders of the indigenous people encountered by Columbus.

cada puerco tiene su sábado Expression that translates to "every pig has his Saturday," referring on one level to the slaughter of a pig, and on another level to a comeuppance.

el Caribe The Caribbean.

Catalán Language of Cataluña, a region of Spain; the reference here is to the Spanish Civil War.

chupacabras Literally, a goatsucker; a mythical creature, perhaps extraterrestrial or supernatural, said to prey on animals in Puerto Rico.

Clemente, Roberto Hall of Fame baseball player from Puerto Rico who died in a plane crash delivering relief supplies to earthquake victims in Nicaragua.

cocodrilo Crocodile.

coco frío In Puerto Rico, a green coconut chilled, then cut open to drink the milk.

colibrí Hummingbird.

compañero Good friend; the word may also refer to a lover, or have connotations of political comradeship.

conga Tall drum of African origin.

conjunto Literally, a musical group; here, a reference to Chicano folk music of South Texas, which features the accordion.

Connolly, James Labor organizer, writer, and leader of the 1916 Easter Rising in Ireland against the British, who was subsequently executed.

cordillera Mountain chain.

Cuba, Joe Bugalú songwriter and bandleader.

cuero Skin of an animal; refers here to the skin of a roasted pig.

danza Elegant dance form originating with the nineteenth-century upper class in Puerto Rico.

Día de los Muertos Day of the Dead, or All Souls day, especially as commemorated in México.

Diario Latino Literally, the Latin Daily; opposition newspaper in El Salvador.

Dios te ama "God loves you."

dominicano Dominican.

dónde está La Revolución "Where is the Revolution?" or, here, "Where is Revolution Street?" (in Tijuana).

durito Literally, "hard little one"; refers here to the scarabs of México.

en la calle San Sebastián On Saint Sebastian Street, in Old San Juan, Puerto Rico.

Española Also spelled as Hispaniola; the name given by Columbus and the conquerors to the island now divided into the Dominican Republic and Haiti. Columbus was governor of the island.

Fajardo Port city on the northeast coast of Puerto Rico.

flamboyán Tree with red blossoms, common in Puerto Rico.

Guánica Town where U.S. troops landed to invade Puerto Rico in the Spanish-American War of 1898.

guatemalteco Guatemalan.

guayabera Long embroidered shirt, common in the Caribbean.

guerrilleros Guerrilla fighters.

Hernández Refers here to the great Puerto Rican composer, Rafael Hernández.

hidalgo Lesser Spanish nobility, many of whom followed Columbus to the New World.

hijo de puta Son of a whore.

indio Indian.

Isabela The capital of Española, founded in the mid-1490s and abandoned a few years later; named for the Queen of Spain.

Jayuya Town in the mountains of Puerto Rico.

jíbaro Puerto Rican term for peasant.

Lares Town in the mountains of Puerto Rico that was the site of a historic rebellion against Spain in 1868, called the Grito de Lares, an event still commemorated today.

machetero Machete-wielder or canecutter.

mambo Cuban song and dance form, popular in the 1950s and 1960s.

Marcantonio, Vito Congressman from New York in the 1930s and 1940s associated with radical causes, including independence for Puerto Rico; an attorney, he represented Soto Vélez and other Nationalists.

Marcos, Subcomandante Spokesman for the contemporary Zapatista movement in México.

marimba A xylophone, indigenous to Central America.

más allá Literally, "further away."

mexicano Mexican.

La Migra Immigration and Naturalization Service.

Miles, General Nelson General of the U.S. Army who led the invasion of Puerto Rico in the Spanish-American War in 1898.

mole Mexican chili sauce, often made with chocolate.

muerte Death.

Neruda, Pablo Nobel Prize–winning poet of Chile; politically persecuted by the government, Neruda became a fugitive in 1948.

oye Literally, "listen"; the equivalent of "hey."

Oye Como Va Literally, "listen to how it goes"; the name of Tito Puente's most famous song.

pa'l carajo Strong Spanish obscenity, of obscure origin and virtually untranslatable.

pandereta Handheld drum used with the plena song form of Puerto Rico.

pastor pentecostal Pentecostal minister.

patrón Landowner or boss.

pegao From "pegado," literally "stuck," referring in particular to the crunchy rice stuck at the bottom of the pot.

plátano Plantain.

plena Song and dance form originating with the Black population of Ponce, Puerto Rico.

Ponce City on the southern coast of Puerto Rico, and the site of the Ponce Massacre, the killing of pro-independence marchers by police, on Palm Sunday, 1937.

La Princesa Literally, "the princess"; a jail in San Juan, where Clemente Soto Vélez began his incarceration in 1936.

Puente, Tito Celebrated Puerto Rican composer, bandleader, and player of the timbales; among the founders of salsa and Latin jazz in New York.

puertorriqueño Puerto Rican.

Río Sucio The "Dirty River" in Nicaragua.

salsa Popular dance music that evolved in the Latino community of New York in the late 1960s.

samba Brazilian song and dance form popularized in the United States by Carmen Miranda during the 1940s.

San Miguel Saint Michael, patron saint of Utuado, Puerto Rico.

Santa Anna, Antonio López de General who led the Mexican Army against the North American invasion of Texas in 1836, including the Battle of the Alamo; in 1838, he lost his leg in battle, and staged an elaborate funeral for the severed limb.

ser o no ser To be or not to be.

Taíno Original indigenous inhabitants of Puerto Rico, decimated by the Spanish.

tamarindo Tamarind tree; such a tree was planted by Albizu in the plaza of Lares to symbolize the cause of independence.

tiburón Shark; also the name of a popular salsa song.

tigres Tigers.

timbales A pair of metal drums with two tuned cowbells; used in salsa or Latin jazz.

toque de queda Curfew.

tormenta Storm.

tumba Grave or tomb.

Utuado Town in the mountains of Puerto Rico, where the author's father was born in 1930.

Veracruz Port city on the central Gulf Coast of México.

mi vida My life; sometimes serves as an expression of endearment, as here.

la vida eterna "Eternal life."

Vieques Offshore island municipality of Puerto Rico, inhabited by more than 9,000 people, which has for decades been the site of live bombardment and war games by the U.S. Navy, leading to high rates of cancer, unemployment, and poverty.

Virgen de Guadalupe Mythical religious figure native to México, representing a synthesis of Catholic and Indian religious beliefs.

Viva Puerto Rico Libre Long live a free Puerto Rico; an expression associated with the movement for independence.

Vocero, El Literally, an advocate or spokesperson; here, a sensationalist newspaper in Puerto Rico.

El Yunque Rain forest in Puerto Rico, noted for its waterfalls.

Zapata, Emiliano Famed revolutionary leader, who fought for agrarian reform and the rights of peasants in the Mexican Revolution of 1910.

zapateado Dance step similar to flamenco, associated here with the "son jarocho" song form of Veracruz, México.

Zapatista Contemporary revolutionary movement based in Chiapas, México, and named for Emiliano Zapata.

Biographical Note

Martín Espada was born in Brooklyn, New York, in 1957. He has published seven collections of poems, most recently *A Mayan Astronomer in Hell's Kitchen* (Norton, 2000). *Imagine the Angels of Bread* (Norton, 1996) won an American Book Award and was a finalist for the National Book Critics Circle Award. Another volume, *Rebellion is the Circle of a Lover's Hands* (Curbstone, 1990), won both the PEN/Revson Fellowship and the Paterson Poetry Prize. His poems have appeared in *The New York Times Book Review*, *Harper's*, *The Nation*, *The Pushcart Prize*, and *The Best American Poetry*. He has published a collection of essays, *Zapata's Disciple* (South End Press, 1998), which received an Independent Publisher Book Award, and is also the editor of *El Coro: A Chorus of Latino and Latina Poetry* (University of Massachusetts Press, 1997), recipient of a Myers Outstanding Book Award. A former tenant lawyer, Espada is a professor in the Department of English at the University of Massachusetts-Amherst. In 2000 he was named the first Poet Laureate of Northampton, Massachusetts.

Index